I0830192

The Stone Thrower

Eric R Spain

Book Title Copyright © 2018 by Eric R Spain and Donkey Two Tales. All Rights Reserved.

All rights reserved. No part of this book may be reproduced in any form or by any electronic or mechanical means including information storage and retrieval systems, without permission in writing from the author. The only exception is by a reviewer, who may quote short excerpts in a review.

Cover designed by Cliky Mouse Productions

The Stone Thrower

Book Three

Contents

About the Author

HI THERE. I TRUST YOU ARE WHERE YOU WANT TO BE. As the front cover of my story reveals, my name is Eric Spain, but sometimes I also go by the pen name of Donkey Two Tales particularly, when writing fairytales. Precociously, the idea to use a pen name such as Donkey Two Tales when writing fairytales is because animals talk in cartoons, don't they? So, why can't they write fairytales about themselves?

Anyway, about me. I was born in a renowned gold mining town called Kalgoorlie, in 1960, which is situated about six hundred kilometers or three hundred and seventy miles north east of Perth, the capital city in Western Australia. I would list all of my academic achievements, but I do not have any. It's not that I didn't attend college, I did however, it didn't suit my lifestyle of wanting to experience everything firsthand, so I threw my cards into the sky of fate and dropped out.

Eventually, after a failed marriage and being involved in business and accounting for about fifteen years, I was speaking to a bank executive one day in April 2002, when he suggested I was in the wrong vocation. He had read my letters concerning a couple of bank agents and their escapades in 2001, and found them descriptive as well as entertaining so, he suggested I should become a writer. And that is exactly what I did, only it took another sixteen years before I had enough assurance to publish my story.

Another reason it took so long however, is interesting because most of that time I spent researching and investigating the subject matter to ensure my claims would stand up to scrutiny. This required a few court appearances to test certain theories, as well as learning what one can or can't do. Thus, after sixteen years of research my story can now be told. But a positive from the trials and tribulations is the reader can be assured that an author definitely knows what he is talking about plus, he also has the evidence to prove what he does say is true. Nevertheless, there is a reason and purpose for presenting my story.

I guess this question has been asked on thousands of occasions and if not, probably millions. So where were you on the morning of 11 September 2001? Well, I can tell you that down under it was 12 September and I was asleep. Yep, that's right, sound asleep until my phone rang at about ten am. It was a friend and he told me to turn on the television, after explaining what happened of course. I was totally shocked and lost for words as I couldn't believe what I was seeing. But sadly and devastatingly, it was true as the day is twenty-four hours long.

And as we know, over the next couple of years more terrorist attacks happened in different parts of the world including Bali, which really hit home because many of the casualties were Australians. I believe it was this moment that Australians really sensed a connection with New York in so much as how we felt and how a city had suffered. And even now I find it emotional thinking and writing about those events. But I also have strong reasons for writing about the attacks because I want to change the world in a profound way.

"So what, everyone wants to change the world," you might say. However, whilst this may very well be true, does everyone have the tools and skillset to make a sincere difference I would ask? By this I mean what good is walking on the moon if nothing changes on earth, because man is still killing the innocent in the name of God? We can invent amazing things, fly to wonderful places, and lift our standard of living to a level of unbelievable comfort, but what value are these changes when we allege damnation and kill in God's name because the wicked must be punished for their sins?

This is the reason for my story and it also informs you about me at the same time I suspect, because if one says they can do something grand and they do it, you know they mean what they say. You see, what good is it to walk on the moon or have all the good things in life unless everyone has the same opportunity? And perhaps the most important thing anyone can do is make the world think about where it is going.

Thus, what price peace? What would you be willing to do to reset the balance of scales and create a situation where the world can have a brand-new start? It is what this story is about, because it involves you the reader, being able to change the world in the most amazing and profound way. Twenty years ago, I was given the tools for this to happen, but didn't know I had them until 28 February 2003. **Yours faithfully...**

Eric R Spain

Introduction

God will judge me on Iraq, says Blair
—The Sydney Morning Herald 5 March 2006

CCORDING TO WESTERN SOCIETY religion does not form part of the law. Therefore, in simplicity, if anyone contravenes the law then obviously, they cannot say "God made me do it," because religion is not a lawful excuse or cause. But can God or religion be used as a constitutional cause or excuse? Generally, because constitutions are not only just about the law, for they take the population's values and beliefs into account, is it possible or acceptable on a political level to say, "God made me do it"? And because constitutional paragraphs or sections are superior to parliamentary statutes, would this be a proper defence for a leader of say, a country in relation to a dubious action or decision?

This book is about the right to judge or what constitutes a lawful defence when it involves Royalty, Presidents, and Prime Ministers. And when I say the right to judge, it's in the context of only *God can judge me*, or *God will judge me*, in relation to justice must not only be done, but it must also be seen to be done. With emphasis on the word *seen* because the outcome should be in this world and not the next. Therefore, this book's subject matter concerns 9/11 and Iraq, but in the context of two wrongs don't make it right.

And it also bases itself on the present tense rather than an historical notion, in the context of a suffix. Hence, the emphasis on what is the current, rather than what took place at a given point in time. For example; relied upon is past tense whilst relying on is gerund or a present participle that has a starting point, but an end to the process is open, or it will continue until such time as another arrangement is made.

The story is also about having to prove your faith in front of the world unsupported by everyone except God. Obviously, if the world doesn't know your story, in defence it is also understandable that is doesn't support you. However, the previous isn't what I am referring to rather, it is having to announce who you are knowing condemnation, ridicule, laughter, and so on are going to be a byproduct from your story.

However, sometimes to prove facts and make the change that is required someone has to make a sacrifice. And in this instance, after fighting with my conscience for a number of years it seems fate and God have pushed me into a corner where, in order to survive I must come forward. Nevertheless, perhaps the most annoying part of this ordeal is because of others I have been forced to live a life not of my choosing, for I would much rather be like everyone else. And those others are not ordinary people, as they occupy positions in society where their decisions affect the entire population, but unlike heroes we dream about, their fame and fortune are built on the lies they tell.

Therefore, this story is set out so you the reader, have the choice between a closed mind or providing an answer to a question of what would you do. For example, if the real God came knocking on your door wanting you to present the truth would you reveal it, deny your faith, or hide in a closet and pretend that you are not available for the undertaking?

Accordingly, the book begins with the question of who has the right to judge and explains a journey of what caused the reasons for that judgement. And considering the story is about me, speaking from experience I can honestly say it wasn't a pleasant journey, and it may become an even worse future. However, if you consider a story with an open mind you will understand I have no choice in any decision I make because either way, it all leads back to one name and He does not negotiate.

Instead He wants, He demands, He antagonises, He annoys, and He interrupts twenty-four hours a day until you obey His Commands. I just wish it was someone else instead of me, but sadly it wasn't so eventually, I have done what He has wanted me to do. For that reason, here is His judgement on Christianity and Islam but equally, my judgement of Almighty God.

The Right to Judge

Bush: God told me to invade Iraq
—Independent 7 October 2005

WHO SETS THE MORAL COMPASS OF A DEMOCRATIC NATION? Maybe the parameters are set by the general majority of the population, or its ethics are set in stone by measures such as the law or a constitution. Obviously, if a nation's ethics are set in stone by the law or constitution, enforcement would just be a matter of application through the courts. And enforcing statutes via the courts can be achieved in a number of ways including by an approved authority, a civil cause, or an application comprising of both criminal and civil in nature, by an approved authority and civilian simultaneously.

Consequently, perhaps the morals of a democratic nation are set in several ways. Firstly, by its constitution secondly, by its parliament and thirdly, by the tolerances of society at any given point in time. Nevertheless, who sets the moral compass for God? By this I mean if there is a situation where God has interfered to prevent something from happening and subsequently, a similar event arises but He does not intervene, then who judges Him?

For example; in relation to 9/11, has there been a situation in the past where God has interfered to prevent an attack of a terrorist nature? And by intervening, I mean if not for His intervention then an attack would have been successful. Also, it must be a situation where only He could have prevented the success of an operation through His influence or warning, whether it is by a messenger or otherwise. Therefore, it must have been an event where circumstances attribute God as the rescuer.

Researching the Bible or Qur'an doesn't reveal much mainly because terrorism in its modern form wasn't invented during those days so the answer isn't there. But there is an event in history that is directly connected to the Bible namely, the King James Version. That event was the Gunpowder plot of 1605, which involved a plan to blow up Parliament as it opened thereby, killing a king, his family, and much of the Protestant aristocracy of England. The idea was to stop the Bible being translated in English and also, put a Catholic on the throne of England.

Fortunately, the plot was foiled when one of the conspirators sent an anonymous letter to a Catholic sympathiser, Lord Monteagle, warning him not to attend the opening of Parliament. The letter said;

"My Lord, out of the love I bear to some of your friends, I have a care of your preservation. Therefore I would advise you, as you tender your life, to devise some escape, to shift your attendance at this parliament. For God and man have concurred to punish the wickedness of this time and think not slightly of this advertisement but retire yourself into your country where you may espy of the event in safety. For though there be no appearance of any stir yet I say they shall receive a terrible blow this parliament and yet they shall not see who hurts them. This counsel is not to be condemned because it may do you good and can do you no harm for the danger is passed as soon as you have burned the letter and I hope God will give you the grace to make good use of it to whose holy protection I commend you."

Lord Monteagle did not burn the letter. Instead he took the letter to the authorities and to the king. This led to a thorough investigation of the buildings the night before Parliament was to open and the discovery of Guy Fawkes, one of the conspirators being found in the cellar with matches alongside 30 barrels of gunpowder that were to be used to kill the king. Plainly, if God wanted His name to be associated with terrorism a letter would have been burnt. Instead, it was the opposite because the letter was the instrument that actually exposed the Gunpowder plot.

The plot is a reliable recording of history where God's name was prevented from being used in conjunction with a terrorist activity. And the influence of God is shown as the issue facing Lord Monteagle at the time was ethics. Fortunately, morality won and a plot was discovered, so the King James Version of the Bible was produced. From this event however, a question has to be asked; since God had previously prevented a terrorist attack through a written message, why didn't He prevent 9/11 in a similar way, such as an anonymous tip off through the media or by some other means?

Could it be that God actually wanted 9/11 to happen? The evidence seems to suggest so because as with the Gunpowder plot, the parameters are the same for the action is one of *God and man concurring to punish the wickedness of this time*. With the cause being an argument between different religions that worship the same God. In relation to the Gunpowder plot, it was the struggle between Catholics and Protestants, or Rome and the Church of England. Whilst 9/11 is between Islam and Christianity, or the East and the West if you like. All of these religions stem from Moses because via Genesis, he was the one who introduced Almighty God to the world. Therefore, if God exists and He prevented the Gunpowder plot, then why didn't He stop 9/11?

Further, the intention of the misconstrued faith from the terrorists of 9/11 was also very similar in nature to the Gunpowder plot, because both attempted to prevent the natural evolution of religion. In the case of the Gunpowder plot, part of its aim was to prevent an English version of the Holy Bible to stop it from being widely read by the average citizen. Whilst in comparison; part of the aim from Al Qaeda was and still is, to install their interpretation of Islam or rid the world of Christ and democracy. Therefore, both events comprise a denial for the average to know a modern God of their time, yet He prevented only one of the events from happening; why is this so?

Why would a God whose written rules include condemnation of murder, and also, who supposedly knows everything and hence, would have known about the 9/11 plan beforehand; not warn those who matter in some form or way? My view is if God is real and He did know about 9/11 beforehand, then He decided not to interfere for a specific reason. That reason is yet to be determined, but in relation to my story, despite its potential to reveal why God chose not to prevent 9/11, suffice to say it has also not been easy writing about it.

Plainly, unless one has confidence it isn't easy writing about yourself particularly, if you do not want to be involved in the subject matter. But unfortunately, sometimes there is no choice. Anyway, the answers to the questions I have sought over the last sixteen years or so encompass why God did not prevent 9/11 from happening. Not that He craves or needs it, but the adulation for God if He ensured the 9/11 plot was discovered before any damage could be done, would have been at record levels. It may have restored an entirely new confidence in the faith and truth of God, Government, and Church. Although, experience has taught me that a part of the reason of God not interfering is He may have unfairly disadvantaged the Islamic religion.

So His decision, or lack of intervention, may have hinged on God not creating an unfair advantage for one religion over another. And by electing no involvement, an opportunity has arisen or had arisen for either side of religion to verify their claims as to which version of faith is true.

And whilst I am no theologist, it seems strange God would act inconsistently in relation to martyrdoms borne from a religion with no forgiveness rule. I mean why change now, or why allow several martyrdoms, which involved thousands of victims when the past says one sacrifice is all that was required; if Allah wanted a forgiveness rule for the Qur'an. Unless the stories of Christ are actually untrue. Allowing for Islam through its prophet and Qur'an, where it is written that there is only one God and He does not have a son, daughter, or wife of course.

These are the questions I posed to myself many years ago, because I could not understand why the same God (Allah) would act one way in a similar religious incident several hundred years ago, and then do a backflip in 2001. And the way to understand this is through Jesus Christ. If Christ does not exist, then surely the Gunpowder Plot would have been successful. But if He does exist, why didn't He protect His martyrdom or own forgiveness rule and warn of 9/11?

Further, despite the Qur'an saying there is only one God, if Allah did sanction 9/11 then why or for what purpose did He allow it because nothing has changed? It's the walking on the moon scenario isn't it, because a great event happened, but man still did not change? So if you are a great God, what is your reason for 9/11? But please do not tell me it was to punish the wicked, for every Muslim is also guilty of something.

Pointedly, this is the crux of the matter. God must go on trial for murder. However, before a reader considers one has lost their marbles please think again, for aside from the Act of Christ, there are at least two other stories in the Bible where man has judged God. The first story is called the Book of Job and he judged God over his treatment. Job was rich, led an exemplary life, and was faithful to God, yet his life was torn apart for no reason other than a test of faith. Job found God guilty of not protecting him. The end result was God restored Job's life tenfold because he was right.

The second story is the Book of Revelation because there is a vision that provides an opportunity in the future, where judgement is made concerning a godlike beast and prophet who did many, or will do many miracles during their time on earth. Hence, judging God is not that far-fetched because there are precedents for referral.

Notwithstanding democratic societies generally tolerate a religious belief in almost anything in today's world, in relation to 9/11, the fact remains that if there is a God then He must be held accountable for the actions of His followers or faith. And as illogical as this may seem, if that God is true and just, then in my view He would allow such a process to prove His innocence or a sound reason for the heinous action.

Anyway, putting aside the previous, in August 2001, I had returned to Queensland on the Gold Coast where I lived, after attending two meetings with a bank's senior executive in Western Australia concerning a number of failings. These issues had been occurring for a several years and were strange because it appeared as if someone in the bank was attempting to keep something hidden. Therefore, before continuing with our judgement of God scenario, the next chapter outlines what made me look at things in another way, which after travelling the hard road, eventually led me to present the conclusions outlined in this book.

His Calling Card

The truth is that killing innocent people is always wrong
– and no argument or excuse, no matter how deeply
believed, can never make it right.
—Imam Feisal Abdul Rauf

O N 16 AUGUST 2001, I ATTENDED A MEETING WITH Richard Lorraway, the National Australia Bank's Senior Executive in Western Australia at the time. It came about because of two facsimiles I had sent to the bank's CEO listing a number of complaints, including unethical and unprofessional behavior, which was and still is outside company policy, and the (Cth) Banking Act 1959.

However, the reality was the issues had actually began on 08 January 1999, until it came to a head in July 2001, where I felt that I could not trust anyone inside the bank in Western Australia therefore, after relocating to the Gold Coast in Queensland, I decided to write to the Chief Executive Officer and inform him of the situation. But before continuing with my story, I want you to consider the start and end dates of the issues with the bank. 08 January 1999 and 16 August 2001, the birth and death of a king; Elvis Presley. In August 2001, I began noticing strange things that appeared to be constantly surrounding my situation. It was surreal.

At the time even some of my friends and associates had been remarking how crazy my life was becoming. And they weren't referring to the state of mind, but rather their reference was in relation to the unusual things that seemed to keep happening for no apparent reason, other than I was the only consistency. Like I said it was surreal, but although I did not know it at the time, the reasons behind my circumstances would become apparent in the not too distant future.

As I have stated the issues began in January 1999, when on behalf of my employers MGY Accounting, I had agreed in principle to the purchase of another accounting practice called Mountford Chartered Accountants. The idea was to increase our fees by another five hundred thousand per annum or thereabouts through purchasing another practice. That way we would almost double our turnover and provide security for our employees in the long term. I was also comfortable with the arrangement because both accounting practices used the same bank and also, shared the same business banking manager therefore, since I trusted the National, things seemed secure.

My mistake. After settlement we soon discovered that the fees of the practice were fraudulently inflated, the former owner had been put into bankruptcy, and many of his former clients were still waiting on their taxation assessments to be lodged. The former owner had also lost his tax agency status, and the bank had been dishonouring his cheques on a regular basis, but again these secrets were not revealed by him or by the bank before settlement. And in point, when I asked our bank manager if there were any issues with the practice, he denied knowledge, despite being the one who had the authority to honour cheques or not, for the former owner.

The accounting practices, that is the one we already owned and the one we had supposedly purchased; were situated in the city of Bunbury, Western Australia, which is about 170 kilometres or 105 miles south west of Perth. I say supposedly purchased because as it turned out, shortly after settlement we were not sure of what we had actually bought. However, after we had taken stock of our situation, we worked out that because I had structured the purchase on a half now and half in twelve months basis, the amount of fees generated by the new practice covered about half of what we had actually borrowed, which was three hundred and fifty thousand dollars.

So it wasn't the end of the world, but it also wasn't great. Then about six months or thereabouts after settlement, we received a letter from the trustees in bankruptcy for the previous owner enquiring about the balance of the sale contract. They were a Chartered Accounting firm called PricewaterhouseCoopers. Obviously, the letter meant I wasn't impressed because there was no way that we were going to pay another dollar to anyone or anybody, so I engaged our lawyer to look at the situation. As a result, he referred us to a Trade Practices Barrister, who took care of everything because after one letter, we never heard from the trustees again. However, once again keep the name of the trustees in mind because we did hear from them in another capacity.

Anyway, after everything had settled down somewhat, I was at a social gathering in a hotel in Bunbury when I noticed our firm's lawyer was also in attendance. Hence, I managed to get his attention because I wanted to discuss a few outstanding small issues associated with the purchase that were annoying. Things like some of the office furniture and so on that we thought was ours, actually belonged to a finance company, which meant we had to honour the debt. The reason I decided to talk about these issues with our lawyer at a social function was to save costs of course. In other words, I knew we were going to be charged some money, but it would be nominal because after all, we were at a hotel and he couldn't charge us for his drinking time.

Nonetheless, as we were chatting about things in general, our lawyer remarked that he thought there was something strange about the settlement and circumstances behind it. Like me, he couldn't believe that the bank would not know about the status or financial health of the practice we had purchased but on the other hand, to prove it would be improbable and if not, impossible. Unless of course one was a fly on the wall I distinctly remember him saying because I responded by saying or a mouse perhaps. And that's when he told me it could be a good idea. Thus, be a mouse and notice little things, but also keep an eye on the bigger picture.

So I took his advice and started being a mouse, because by this stage of my life I had extensive business and accounting experience therefore, I knew what he meant and how to go about it. Obviously, my position in our firm wasn't that of an accountant rather, I was the firm's manager and aside from administrative duties, my role was to increase the fees by getting new clients. Hence, after our discussion, it was upward and onward for me, which meant I set out to bring in enough new business to recover our losses from settlement whilst also, keeping a mouse eye on the bank.

Therefore, I targeted the commercial market of Perth because being the capital city it was the biggest and easiest pool to gain new clients from. Also, Bunbury was only a two-hour slow drive away thus, distance would not be an insurmountable stumbling block preventing success. And as it turned out my plan worked because we started getting new clients and our turnover increased markedly.

Although unfortunately, after almost twelve months of constantly being away, my marriage became a casualty because no matter how hard I tried, on far too many occasions I couldn't be there when it mattered. At this time I also noticed a difference in my feelings, for whilst things weren't the same simultaneously, I didn't really care.

Initially, I put my strained relationship down to being away and the stress of fixing a mess, which I later found out was actually caused by an ugly bank. But deep down, I knew I had changed and there was no turning back from the path I was on.

Nevertheless, I continued with my endeavours and by this time I had been working with a new client when he offered me an opportunity that I gleefully took. Because business was good, I had set up an office in Perth to save travelling constantly, and had been looking at increasing turnover through a purchase to fund my expenses and take the burden off the accounting practice in Bunbury. Therefore, I set up a private company called Burymore Pty Ltd, to separate the accounting practice from other business interests and opportunities that were increasingly coming my way.

The spinoff for the accounting practice was they would get all of the administrative and tax work, but I would own or have one hundred percent of the profits generated by business interests and other opportunities. So this client offered me a deal where he had a parcel of land that encompassed part of a swamp in a soon to be rezoned area. He wanted his original purchase price in cash, and the balance of its valuation was going to be satisfied by an issue of shares in my private company, Burymore.

It was a good deal for both parties because the plan was to purchase a tavern with the left-over equity after settlement. Then sell the land after rezoning, which would extinguish any debt our company had thereby, leaving it with a healthy bank account and some real purchasing power if another opportunity arose. The reason why he liked the idea was because his business was asset heavy and didn't have a huge cash flow, so by investing in my company he would be getting a good return on his investment and a substantial share of future profits thereby, providing another income stream. The land was called Hope Valley, its size was about 125 000 square metres, and it was going to be rezoned from rural to industrial property.

Therefore, I arranged a meeting with our business banking manager Mr Ripp, and presented my plan. The bank approved my loan application, settlement was executed, and things were looking fantastic. If only everyone kept to their end of the bargain of course. Unfortunately, things did not turn out this way because once again it appeared someone in the bank wasn't doing what they were supposed to be doing, or something unexplainable was causing grief. And to be honest, even today I am sort of in two minds, for I still can't believe bank servants and accountants were that dumb, but the evidence says they were.

What happened was I had put in an offer on a tavern called the E Bar in a suburb called West Perth, which was a commercial area right next to the city. Anyway, during the due diligence process, I discovered the business owed more than the price I was prepared to offer. Normally, when it gets to that stage a potential buyer would decline the sale contract. However, the company that owned the tavern also owned another business called Liars Saloon, which was very profitable.

Therefore, rather than cancel the sale contract, I suggested to the directors of the company, which owned the two taverns, that investing in their company would be an option. Thereby, they would get financial stability and still be part owners, whilst in theory I would get two taverns for the price of one. Everyone agreed, so I arranged another meeting with the bank to see if it would be a problem. And after a very positive meeting with the bank, I was confident in the change of direction. By this stage it was October 2000, and a good business plan was beginning to come to fruition.

The situation was; the land was going to be rezoned so its value was going to increase from about nine hundred thousand dollars to around three million dollars. Total debt between the two taverns and my private company at the time was almost nine hundred thousand dollars. The value of the two taverns was about seven hundred thousand dollars. So simple balance sheet math says three million dollars minus nine hundred thousand dollars is two million one hundred thousand dollars net value.

But taking it one step further, because the government wanted to resume the land it meant that a quick sale or turnaround was an option. And quick in real estate terms for land of this type meant six months or thereabouts. Further, as an incentive for a quick sale, it also wasn't necessary to settle for the full industrial value of the land as an amount of two million dollars would have been sufficient. Thus, the incentive was the government saves a million dollars, and we extinguish our total debt in less than a year. Therefore, we would own two profitable taverns and have almost a million dollars cash in our bank account.

More to the point, rather than the accounting firm in Bunbury owing the bank money, we could have taken over the debt and everything would have been paid, with three hundred thousand dollars still in the bank providing good working capital and sound financial stability for the taverns and accounting business. That way, the government wins, the bank wins, and we win, so everyone is satisfied. Unfortunately, sometimes the left hand doesn't tell the right hand what is going on so problems arise.

After getting approval from the bank for an increase in funds and adjustment of the business plan to invest in the company that owned the two taverns, we began refurbishing the bar in West Perth. This meant closing it and covering any losses and other expenses, as well as the cost of refurbishment. And on an administration level the only thing left to do was to dot the I's and cross the T's. But like I have said, if the left hand doesn't tell right what is going on, problems arise.

One of those problems was by mid-December 2000, I still hadn't executed any new loan agreements with the bank and we were several hundred thousand dollars above our overdraft limit. Of course in the mean time I had been communicating with the manager, who kept on assuring me that everything was approved, but due to his work load settlement would be delayed however, do not worry. Then about a week later I noticed that our overdraft was way below its limit because there was a deposit of two hundred and fifty thousand dollars in the trading account. The deposit's reference revealed a short-written explanation saying; *awaiting new deal.*

Obviously, I assumed that the deposit was from the new financial arrangement so settlement should only be a matter of days. But by the end of December 2000, still no paperwork and once again the overdraft is way over its limits. So I reviewed the bank statements again and noticed two hundred and fifty thousand dollars had been taken out of the trading account about a week or just under after it was deposited. By this stage I am confused therefore, I contacted the senior business banking manager of the bank's Homemaker Centre in Bunbury, Mr Hallet, to explain the problem.

As a result, we arranged a meeting to be held in his office to discuss the issues and for me to explain the business plan, which confused me because they had a copy and I thought they would know how to read, so what was the problem? Anyway, I went to a meeting and after being told by Mr Hallet that he was unaware of what our business banking manager was doing, I began to explain a simple business plan. You know, sell land as the government wanted to resume it, pay off the debt, everybody is happy.

His response was positive because before I finished my presentation he told me that I knew what I was doing and therefore, the bank would be in touch. Or carry on regardless and in the meantime the bank would organise the long overdue paperwork, so settlement could take place and everyone would be on the same page. But as per usual someone got their wires crossed somewhere because in February 2001, I received a letter from the bank advising my account was referred to its credit section.

The letter advised that a Mr Bob Jacobs of the bank's Asset Structuring Department would be in contact with me shortly. And true to the letter's words, in March 2001, Mr Jacobs contacted me and we arranged a meeting at the bank's head branch in the city. I also informed that I would be bringing our financial controller to the meeting, more for my protection than anything else I might add.

Have you ever been associated with a project where it seems everyone else involved are just plain incompetent? Well I have. A logical person would find my situation very difficult to grasp for at the meeting with the bank, Mr Jacobs opened a file and began listing the debt level however, the file and its debt load was not me or my private company rather, it was another bank client altogether. By this stage frustration was relevant nevertheless, I sat patiently whilst Mr Jacobs excused himself and went to get the right account file.

A short while after, he returns but has no paperwork or file. Then he apologises and suggests that if I am right about my plan and the land, the bank would not have a problem however, would I agree to have an independent investigating accountant, appointed by the bank no less; analyse the business. This included the two taverns, land, and business plan. I agreed because I knew I was right and thus, had no fears as to whether the direction I had taken would stand up to scrutiny. Hence, the meeting ended with Mr Jacobs providing me with his business card.

About a week later, I received a letter from the bank informing Mr Martin Jones of Ferrier Hodgson Chartered Accountants, had been appointed as the investigating accountant into the business affairs of my private company Burymore Pty Ltd. And again I still had nothing to fear because aside from a good business plan, I knew who Mr Jones was because our paths had crossed before in an unrelated business situation, so after his investigation I felt it would be full steam ahead. Consequently, I contacted Mr Jones and arranged a meeting.

By this time it was early April 2001, and both taverns were operational, with a newly refurbished E Bar steadily increasing its daily turnover. Thereby, at the meeting with Mr Jones I outlined my plan, and confirmed that both taverns were operational and soon their combined turnover would be able to service our debt until such time as the land was sold to the government. However, I also said that we still required about thirty thousand dollars to finish paying for the refurbishment.

The meeting ended with Mr Jones being very positive by confirming that he would contact the bank on our behalf to secure the funds required. I left the meeting feeling upbeat, because through our discussions I was confident that finally we were getting somewhere, and once again it should only be a short time before normality resumed.

No, wrong again. Two weeks passed and I still had not heard from Mr Jones or Mr Jacobs for that matter and things were becoming critical. Therefore, I rang Mr Jacobs to see if he had heard from Mr Jones, but unfortunately his answer was in the negative, so I rang Mr Jones. Then it was put to me. To protect exposure for Burymore, Mr Jones suggested voluntary administration for Jack Corporation, the company which owned the taverns. That way it would be easier for the investigative process, as technically Jack Corporation wasn't the bank's client.

Apparently, the stumbling block with the investigative process was because Jack Corporation wasn't the bank's client. So investigating its financial operations wasn't possible because it was outside Ferrier Hodgson's jurisdiction. This meant the bank would not provide support for Burymore unless Ferrier Hodgson had management control of Jack Corporation. The only way to do this was by voluntary administration. Therefore, being Chairman and CEO of the company it was a matter of me convincing the other directors to agree.

Clearly, I discussed the positives and negatives of taking this course, but the reality was Burymore needed to pay the creditors for the refurbishment, and I was assured that it was only an administrative process, not liquidation. Reluctantly, I agreed, for I could understand the logic behind the suggestion, and considering how things had turned out my choices were limited anyway.

So Jack Corporation was put into voluntary administration. And upon confirmation I contacted Mr Jacobs to discuss the bank's financial support for Burymore namely, thirty thousand dollars required to pay those creditors that were still outstanding concerning the refurbishment. There are moments in your life when you just want to scream because of the built-up frustration from dealing with deceit, incompetence, miscommunication, and so on. I mean we have all been through it haven't we? This was one of those moments because Mr Jacobs denied what Mr Jones told me, and said the bank wasn't providing any support. My response wasn't great however, Mr Jacobs interrupted and said I didn't know what I was doing as he was a Chartered Accountant in charge of the bank's credit department, so he could squash me like a bug.

Squash me like a bug! Consequently, I was rather devastated and after the heated discussion I contemplated where to from here. Therefore, I sought advice from an accountant I knew, because something smelled and he was very good at seeing the truth behind a smokescreen. Our discussion began with a quick explanation of where things were at with the bank and so forth. However, when I mentioned the names Jacobs and Jones, he interrupted and enquired as to why two investigating accountants from Ferrier Hodgson are involved if I was dealing with the bank's credit department.

Being confused I asked what he was talking about, because as far as I was aware Ferrier Hodgson were appointed as independent investigators, and Mr Jacobs was a Chartered Accountant and senior executive in the Asset Structuring Department. But he was adamant that it was the same person from Ferrier Hodgson, because it was the only Bob Jacobs he knew, and the bank outsourced its credit department with seconded employees from first and second tier accounting firms. Then he asked if Mr Jacobs had ever revealed his true employment position, because as far as he was aware the same Mr Jacobs was not the bank's senior executive of anything.

What followed after my conversation about Mr Jacobs can only be described as an effort in madness, for Mr Jones set about liquidating everything whilst also, refusing to respond to my phone calls or return my messages. It began with me being locked out of my office in Subiaco, ended with a fire sale of Liars Saloon in Victoria Park, and closure of the E Bar in West Perth. Hence, Jack Corporation was no more. And the only reason Burymore was still surviving was because the land hadn't been sold.

Subsequently, as I have previously stated in this chapter, I could not trust anyone from the bank in Western Australia, so I gave up arguing and relocated to Queensland where, I developed another business plan, this time it was just for the ugly bank, Mr Jacobs, Mr Jones, and Ferrier Hodgson. Initially, I sent two facsimiles to the bank's CEO with the first letter listing my complaints, whilst the second asked if a CEO knew why elephants were scared of mice. The second facsimile included a copy of a bank statement which showed two hundred and fifty thousand dollars being credited and then debited from Burymore's trading account.

As a result, I received a reply from a customer service manager asking for me to contact the bank's Senior Executive of Asset Structuring in Western Australia namely, Mr Richard Lorraway. And as I have already stated at the beginning of this chapter, a meeting was held on 16 August 2001. This also meant a flight to Western Australia.

The First Lie

No religion on earth condones the killing of innocent
people, no faith tradition tolerates the random killing of
our brothers and sisters on this earth.
—Imam Feisal Abdul Rauf

IT WAS AN UNEVENTFUL FLIGHT, I ARRIVED BACK in Perth about a week before the meeting was due. I had arranged to stay at the residence of a former director of Jack Corporation, which allowed me to prepare as I required a logical explanation to what can only be described as bizarre. In my view I still could not comprehend why the bank would make such drastic decisions, and what possessed a person to misrepresent his true position at the bank. I mean surely, one must lead a fantasy life if they pretend they are someone other than themselves.

Mr Jacobs, what an absolute fool. I can assure you that a true Chartered Accountant does not misrepresent, but this guy he was something else. Obviously, working in the bank's credit department provided him with the atmosphere to express his delusions of grandeur without fear of reprisal, which only shows how out of control an ugly elephant was. Anyway, the week seemed to go by very quickly and it wasn't long before I was enjoying a coffee on St Georges Terrace, whilst looking at two bank servants, and trying to ascertain if they carried guilt or not.

After introductions and small talk, the first question I asked was who is actually in charge of the Asset Structuring Department in Western Australia. Mr Lorraway confirmed it was him however, he did not believe me when I said Mr Jacobs claimed that he was the principal manager in Western Australia, so I produced a letter signed by him that confirmed my allegations. Round one to a mouse.

Then I asked how it was possible to take money from an unrelated bank client's account, deposit it into my account, and several days later reverse the process? My view was that if a customer had money in their account, unless some arrangement had been made beforehand, the bank should not be able to touch it. And I assume that every customer would feel the same otherwise, where is the security of any deposit a person makes to the ugly elephant bank?

Both bank representatives looked at each other, and almost in unison, nodded their heads in the affirmative and said, "flying kites." Now I do not know about those of you who are reading this story, but how is it possible for any bank to fly kites? So I enquired as to what they meant. Mr Lorraway explained that it was a slang term used in banking circles to describe a business banking manager that wants to prevent the credit department from seeing unauthorised overdraft excesses.

Mr Lorraway went on to explain that when an overdraft stays above its limit for a certain period of time, to avoid audit indicators managers transfer money from an unrelated account into the problem account for several days. Then after the audit period has passed the processed is reversed, so the money goes back into the unrelated account. He did say that there was no risk to the client because the bank guaranteed the deposits anyway.

Importantly, it was also revealed that I wasn't the only one whose account bank servants Ripp and Hallet had been performing the unauthorised flying maneuvers on. But by this stage I was perplexed, for I didn't care how they described it, because their pilots weren't very good at flying anyway, as bank kites were crashing everywhere and destroying the business lives of innocent clients.

Further, I asked how it was possible for a seconded employee, such as Mr Jacobs, was able to farm out jobs to the firm that he really worked for. Particularly considering Ferrier Hodgson's real or purported expertise was in administration and liquidation, and that Mr Jones was a senior partner at the firm. My concern was how is this not a conflict of interest if it involves a seconded employee in the bank's asset structuring department, who is secretly passing out jobs to his real employer or boss?

Moreover, I continued by asking why the bank did not have proper business cards that disclosed if an employee was permanent or seconded. I mean obvious words on the business cards should have said 'seconded manager' thereby, preventing potential conflicts of interests and informing clients of who they were dealing with.

Anyway, the outcome of the meeting was the bank agreed to an advance of twenty thousand dollars to assist with personal losses I had the displeasure of experiencing via crashing elephant kites. And we agreed to meet the next day to discuss a settlement arrangement which involved me buying a business in Queensland and the bank heavily discounting the debt owed on the land. However, considering the bank's track record, I wasn't confident on its intentions or settlement. And I was right because it took less than three months before the bank's seconded employee kite scheme crashed again.

Two days later I flew back to Queensland, and upon returning to my apartment on the Gold Coast, I was pleasantly surprised when I noticed a drawing of a pretty woman on my dining table, with a note thanking me for allowing friends to stay. The picture was drawn by the wife of a friend. She was quite the accomplished artist, and we were friends because her husband used to work for MGY Accounting in Bunbury. I was also the master of ceremonies at their wedding so I really did appreciate the thought behind the drawing. Therefore, I hung it above my office desk, where I was soon to write many letters to a bank executive.

By this time it was almost at the end of August 2001, and I felt things were looking up, which made me relax somewhat for the next couple of weeks. But then the world watched a heinous crime under the disguise of martyrdom; 9/11. The saddest day in recent US history, and New York felt the brunt of it. As I have already written, I was asleep when Al Qaeda launched its horrific version of martyrdom nevertheless, when I first saw it, my immediate thoughts were, why God? Why would a God do this because to me it was the Gunpowder Plot revisited, only this time it was successful.

Moreover, as far as I was concerned the event was a jackass martyrdom because I was very confident that in three days there would be no spiritual resurrection of any description. Therefore, if God does exist why did He allow such a heinous crime to be committed, when in reality no one is innocent in this world, including Muslims. And I felt sick when I saw pictures of Muslims dancing in the streets of Pakistan, whilst burning American flags in celebration of their victory, and chanting, "Allah is great!" But Al Qaeda had lied to their martyrs because an Islamic Allah is not great at all.

Regrettably, for the next month or so the lead stories everywhere centered on the aftermath of 9/11, which noticeably had many countries on edge, as well as anyone who had to fly somewhere, me included. Understandably, security was tightened and airports became a nightmare when catching a flight.

On the Gold Coast however, a human type mouse was continuing with his escapade against an elephant bank and its wayward servants. Towards the end of October 2001, I had received a fax from the Bunbury accounting practice, which revealed that the bank had engaged an investigating accountant from PricewaterhouseCoopers into the financial affairs of MGY; the company that owned the practice. My immediate thought was here we go again!

PricewaterhouseCoopers were the trustees in bankruptcy for the former owner of the practice that MGY had purchased. And now they were investigating accountants for the bank into the financial affairs of the Bunbury accounting practice? Therefore, I wrote to the bank via its senior executive Mr Lorraway, and reminded him the same trustees in bankruptcy, were also the same investigating accountants who by their association with the bank, made them involved in the original purchase of a business, whose bankrupt owner had fraudulently inflated income to get a higher sale price.

And mentioning of course that the same bank had the same business banking manager, who acted for both parties on the sale contract, but simultaneously he denied knowledge of dishonouring cheques for the former principal and party to the sale. I was flabbergasted, for I had learned that all along the bank had known the accounting practice MGY had purchased could not support any decent sized loan, based on the true figures of its fee income. So irresponsible lending reared its ugly head, and in the middle was a bank and trustee, who also operated out of the bank's credit department.

Therefore, it all made sense, the ugly elephant bank knew beyond doubt that there was something wrong with the purchase, but advanced a loan anyway because as a secured creditor it was first in line to receive any funds from the sale contract between the former principal and MGY Accounting. The problem I had however, was I wasn't a director of MGY Accounting and did not own the business. The only thing the bank wanted from me was a third-party guarantee, but the clause in the loan contract was useless, because Mr Lorraway quickly removed my exposure thereby, preventing me from being able to commence immediate litigation.

PricewaterhouseCoopers also withdrew as the investigating accountants into the affairs of MGY, citing conflict of interest as the reason. A small win, but it wasn't what I was after hence, I rejected the bank's proposed settlement deed in relation to the land and Burymore, then faxed several letters. At this stage time had elapsed, and it was December 2001, therefore I decided to have an enjoyable Christmas in Sydney.

I spent almost two months in Sydney before returning home to the Gold Coast in Queensland. Part of the reason I was away so long was I had sent a letter of complaint to the Australian Competition and Consumer Commission (ACCC) concerning the bank. And whilst it was unfortunate the ACCC could not help, the effect was the bank wanted to attempt another settlement agreement. Therefore, being that it was a very large company and its legal representatives a large firm, the wheels of progress turn slowly so the administration attached to settlement agreements take time to finalise.

Questionably, the problem I had with signing yet another settlement agreement (second one thus far) with the bank, was it wouldn't release the mortgage it had over the land. That is the original amount owing to the bank as at August 2001, was just over a million dollars or thereabouts. So the bank would write off several hundred thousand dollars on the outstanding loan balance, then I had to refinance the land and find a business to purchase so I could meet my obligations. By the time I signed the settlement agreement with the bank in Sydney, the outstanding loan balance was reduced to four hundred thousand dollars.

So I had to find a new financier, despite that my credit rating was shot because of a bank and friends, then I had to borrow the outstanding loan balance plus, whatever a new business cost to effect settlement with the bank. I never understood why the bank just didn't write off the total loan and release the land thereby, providing me with the opportunity to sell it and make a fresh start. Further, if the bank advanced any money it would add that amount on top of the outstanding loan balance on the land, which made things even more difficult. I was in a catch 22 situation, but in my view, the bank was not really trying its best to end the merry go round.

Nevertheless, I returned home to the Gold Coast and set about trying to execute my part of the arrangement. You know, find a financier and business, then settle with the bank so I could move on with my life. Pigs fly too they say and dreams are ten a penny apparently, because it didn't matter what I did there was no way that I could execute my end of the arrangement, unless the land was totally unencumbered.

By this stage I had lost a lot of friends, my family thought I had lost the plot, and the landlord of the former E Bar in West Perth wanted someone's blood for causing the atrocity. All of which meant that I was the scapegoat and an elephant was sitting pretty with is wayward agents creating more damage elsewhere I suspect. So things were getting tough, time was moving on, and there appeared to be no end in sight.

It was Thursday before Easter 2002, I was sitting at my desk in my apartment and began to write yet another letter to the bank when I thought to hell with, and decided to visit the bar a friend had told me about. Called Melbas, the bar was situated on Cavil Avenue in Surfers Paradise. And as bars go, at the time it was the most popular spot in Surfers. With a nightclub upstairs and restaurant bar downstairs, lining up to get in was not unusual.

Generally, not one to drink and drive I caught a taxi to Melbas at around 8 pm, and after paying the driver I made my way to the bar and restaurant. Melbas was quite an impressive place, with a long bar starting from near the reception desk at the main entrance, and winding in a shape similar to the number five I suppose, until it had the effect of dividing the floor space into three main areas. TV screens hung from the support poles strategically placed around the building, whilst in the corner behind the bar was the area where the disc jockey entertained the patrons.

When I arrived it was starting to get busy, but not so hectic that it was difficult to be served. Stepping up to the bar, I noticed one of the staff members had an unusual tattoo of a butterfly near her left front shoulder, just above the breast, but below the neckline. She made her way to serve me and smiled warmly when she asked what I wanted to drink. Pointedly, she also must have seen that I couldn't help but notice the tattoo because she told me that it was a special stick on variety, which confused me somewhat. Then she attempted to have a joke by saying that if I scratched the butterfly it would release a pleasant perfume.

Jokingly, she asked if I wanted to scratch and sniff, to which I declined because I had never heard of any tattoos that could do that, so I felt she was having a bit of a tease. And as the night wore on we continued with many jokes about butterflies and fishing until she asked if I wanted to have a drink with her when she finished her shift.

True to her word, at around 11:30 that evening she made her way to the top end of Melbas, where I was leaning with my back against the bar drinking my sorrows about the bank into temporary oblivion. I noticed that she was quite tall, about five feet ten inches in high heels, but with a slender petite body, and beautiful facial features most models would be envy of. To be honest, I thought stuff Easter because here comes Christmas, but I was brought back into reality when she actually introduced herself as Christine. She then told me that most people called her Chrissie and would like it if I could refer to her as the same.

We talked for the next hour or so about nothing in particular, and everything that mattered in between, until I had to say goodbye because it was late and my brain was pleading with me to stop the punishment and go home. Therefore, we swapped phone numbers and I made my way towards the taxi rank about fifty metres east along Cavil Avenue, where there was an abundance of waiting cabs thirsty for customers.

I didn't return to Melbas or contact Chrissie until about a week after Easter because a friend had come to stay, for we had planned to go to the Byron Bay Blues Festival, so after a few heavy days of entertainment, I was just about worn out. Nevertheless, I also could not get Chrissie's face out of my mind because there seemed to something vaguely familiar about it. A bit like a sense of déjà vu because although her face seemed familiar like an old friend, we had never met before. At the time, whilst it was a little unnerving I also dismissed the sensation as being in a moment.

Soon the days turned into weeks and before long it was early May 2002. Still no real joy with the bank, finding a business was almost impossible and therefore, as my forty second birthday was getting closer, I also began to wonder if a nightmare with an ugly elephant and its crashing kites would end. Meanwhile, the only solace I had was Melbas, Chrissie, and several new friends I was beginning to know because they were also staff members of the bar and generally, joined our drinking party at the end of their respective shifts. We had many laughs but for me, the next morning meant rather than awakening from a dream, instead I was returning to a nightmare again.

Alarmingly, the next bizarre episode happened late at night as I was writing yet another letter to Richard Lorraway listing the reasons for my lack of progress. As one is, I was deep in thought when the ring tone of my phone sprang into life. It was a text message from Chrissie and said; *are you my salvation9?* Now I am not the smartest guy in the world therefore, I do not know everything. However, this was different because I do know what salvation9 means. In biblical terms it means are you my Judge? And right at that moment I felt a chill run through my soul as if I was dancing with Lucifer along the watchtower of hell. I was so frightened, so scared, and so alone. Stunned, my eyes followed the wall around the room.

Then as if frozen by an Antarctic chill, I realised why Christine's face seemed eerily familiar. The picture on the wall was her! It was uncanny, it seemed that since August 2001, her eyes had been looking down at me whenever I typed. With a racing mind and trembling fingers I responded with; *God is your salvation not me.*

Suddenly, I received another message from her, which asked; *are you sure172?* So being one not to ignore the hands of fate I sent a reply; *only God can save your soul.* And as if anticipating that I needed and end to weirdness, she responded; *I see533.* My next move wasn't hard to figure out because I turned the mobile phone off.

Then I sat for a minute, contemplating if I had lost my mind, because now I was sure I was hallucinating, and it would only be a matter of time before men in white coats would be coming to take me away to a farm where life is good apparently. Either that or an urgent end to a bank saga and explanation from Chrissie to prevent me from losing it all, was the medicinal requirement. Therefore, I promised myself that I would personally see Chrissie the next day and ask what the hell she was texting me about.

Part of the reason or full reason perhaps, was I did help her financially when she had a little problem concerning her rent. Her setback was the person who used to share her apartment had a motorbike accident, and she couldn't find someone suitable to share with, so it was either move out or get help with rent. Luckily, I happened to be around at the time maybe, or was it fate building the path I was walking? At the time I didn't know and didn't care really, because I just wanted the weird things to stop, and the first step was to see Chrissie for an explanation.

How wrong I was again, because when I spoke to Chrissie she denied texting me anything. He story was she had fallen asleep, but when she woke the next morning she checked her messages and like me, she also couldn't believe it. I was skeptical of her explanation, but I was also happy because I knew I hadn't lost my mind. Although, I didn't mention the picture because sometimes too much information can be just as damaging as none. Instead, because a few friends were coming to stay with me to celebrate my birthday, I planned to get their opinion on the drawing.

Our intentions were to celebrate at Melbas with dinner first then partying upstairs in the nightclub after. Therefore, they would meet Chrissie anyway, then I would get them to compare the two. However, it didn't get that far because one of those friends made a comment about Chrissie and the drawing the next day without prompting by me. His said he thought I had the drawing done by a street artist, and Chrissie and I were seeing each other on a personal level.

Imagine his surprise when I told him how I came to get the drawing in the first place. Of course some of the others weren't surprised because they had already seen how bizarre my life was becoming hence, carry on regardless.

Nonetheless, notwithstanding the uncanny picture and weird text messages, aside from sending Chrissie the drawing because it was too strange for even me to deal with, the next few months passed without drama. However sadly, the terrorists reared their ugly heads again because exploding bombs in Bali killed many Australians and other tourists holidaying on the island. It was devastating, and once again it seemed the world was being held to ransom by a faith that inspired monstrosity.

As for me, just after the Bali bombings, my patience had finally been torn to shreds hence, I told Mr Lorraway the bank could keep the land. And whilst I had been talking to the government about the price of resumption, I did not want to go through another year of my life haggling with an ugly elephant. Therefore, the bank offered a cash settlement of two hundred thousand dollars in exchange for the land, so I could finally move forward with my life. I wasn't happy, but it was enough for what was required.

I had been looking for a business, and actually found something suitable, if I could find some willing partners. The business was called Mary Street Night Club, and I had worked out that if three other partners joined me, we could put in one hundred and fifty thousand dollars each, purchase the club, and also have one hundred thousand dollars working capital left over to maintain and increase patronage. Obviously, the sale price was five hundred thousand dollars.

Therefore, I executed the settlement agreement with the bank and put a deposit on the club. Unfortunately however, the partners who wanted to be involved could not raise enough capital thereafter, I scrapped the idea and set about doing something on my own for a change. Luckily, the broker who was selling the club had a restaurant on his books, which he told me about and gave me a copy of their trading history for the previous two years. The restaurant was called 29 High Street and it was located in the busy commercial area of Toowong, Brisbane.

By this time I had distanced myself from Chrissie and her friends because it was just too weird and uncomfortable for me considering the text and picture scenario. It wasn't that I did not like her or her friends, but I had a problem and it required fixing, so it was time to move on.

The Second Lie

War is neither glamorous nor attractive. It is monstrous.
Its very nature is one of tragedy and suffering.
—The Dalai Lama

IT WAS FRIDAY EVENING, 28 FEBRUARY 2003, and I was enjoying a quiet drink at the Regatta Hotel in Toowong. Perhaps you could say that I was celebrating a return to normal life particularly, when considering what had fallen into my lap two about months previous. Shortly after executing the final settlement deed with the bank in December 2002, I received a letter from Martin Jones of Ferrier Hodgson, accusing me of insolvent trading as a director of Jack Corporation, as well as demanding several hundred thousand dollars compensation to pay for the outstanding creditors of the company. And if I didn't pay legal action would follow.

Aside for my negotiations with the bank standing for something, the letter from Mr Jones was incorrectly addressed and stated the insolvency began as early as July 1999. Apparently, this was the result of a complete investigation by him and hence, payment was expected. Therefore in January 2002, I responded by sending Mr Jones a letter, which detailed my investigation into his unethical behaviour.

Depending on your career, there are times in your life where you will come across someone who is so silly that their actions defy description. This was one of those times because I was not a director of Jack Corporation in 1999. More importantly, being a mouse type, during fourteen months of verbal and written negotiations with the ugly elephant bank, I had gathered enough evidence to send the partnership of Ferrier Hodgson bankrupt, for I was of the opinion professional indemnity insurance would not cover the unethical behaviour of Mr Jacobs and Mr Jones.

I mean it was more than simple negligence because they had contravened the Banking Act, and the relevant statutes were criminal in nature, so there was no way their insurance company would have to pay anything. Moreover, damning evidence came from both the bank and its other accounting agents PricewaterhouseCoopers, by their written admittance of conflicting interests. Therefore, not only was there a claim for defamation of character, but Ferrier Hodgson would also be liable for the missed opportunities that were laid out in my business plan by causing estoppels. And it was going to be the easiest case to win anyone could imagine, because the evidence was actually supported by an irrefutable deed that was stamped or registered in a court.

So here I was, standing near a window next to the side entrance of the Regatta Hotel, thinking how sweet life was. I had also put down a ten-thousand-dollar deposit on a soon to be happening little restaurant bar, with its renovations and promotional budget being paid for by the dumbness of Jacobs and Jones. I knew the compensation payout would be around twenty million dollars therefore, I was one happy mouse and laughing all the way to the bank so to speak. Life was good indeed.

"Never stand in the way of a girl trying to get to a bar," she said. I still shudder whenever I think or write about this pick-up line. Her comment jolted my solitude like a mermaid singing her song of temptation. Sweet, captivating, and yet deadly. Quickly, I was brought back to reality, for standing in front of me was a vision of an irresistible smile, radiating from an alluring angel who appeared too good to be true, but was. At first I was delighted because I was thinking that life couldn't get any better, but then it did almost immediately after a thought, which I must admit was a little unnerving at the same time, if you can understand my drift.

The unnerving part was it was almost as if someone was reading my thoughts because out of nowhere, the end to my fairytale suddenly appeared. Well I can honestly say that is what I thought at the time because at this moment my story said, mouse takes on an ugly elephant, wins battle, cleans up with the loot, meets his princess, and rides off into the sunset. And they lived happily ever after, right? Wrong again!

Briefly, thinking she is my fairytale, I seized an opportunity and offered to buy her a drink however, she said she was with friends. Therefore, impressions were the order of the day, so I bought her and the friends a drink. And this is where a fairytale ends, for what took place after was the realisation my nightmare was continuing, only this time I had no control because I was soon to become like a puppet on a string.

After buying a round of drinks, and engaging in small talk, she walked away for several minutes before coming back to find out more. At this point, it became quite disconcerting for me. She asked why I was drinking at the Regatta, so I told her that I was thinking of buying a restaurant bar just around the corner. I have deliberately not revealed her name for reasons that will become obvious later plus, her details are really unimportant in relation to the context of this story, and privacy is also paramount.

Anyway after my response, in her enthusiasm to indicate that she wanted me in her future, she told me she knew lots of people and would be able to help with my efforts. Then she asked if she could give me her business card, which although a little cautious, I accepted. However, as she went to look into her bag to find the card, she began having difficulty for it appeared as if she had actually left the cards on her desk at work or something. Unluckily for me, she eventually found one, but before handing a card to me, her facial expression suddenly changed into one of bemusement because apparently it wasn't the right one?

Her response was the card was the right one as the contact details were the same, but wrong because she had been promoted and it reflected her old position rather than her real one. Nevertheless, would I please keep the card anyway because I would still be able to contact her if I needed help. Thereby, she gave me the card, but as she did I noticed two things about it that created confusion in an already overwhelmed mind. The first surprise were the words 'Job Access' on the card, and the second was it had a green jigsaw puzzle piece as its logo. Quiescently at that moment, time appeared to slow down and those around me began moving in slow motion.

I could also see a jigsaw puzzle putting itself together; forming a picture of a road I wanted no part of. So I discouraged further conversation, as I knew I had to get out of there to contemplate running far, far, away. However, at the same time I also knew that no matter how far I ran, I would only be running to stand still consequently, there was no way out and no way back from where I was heading.

I hailed a taxi to take me back to the motel I was staying at meanwhile, as the cab was making its way towards my destination my heart and mind were racing, thinking, then pounding and silently screaming in frustration at the prospect of what I must do. There would be no fairytale at this juncture, and a rocky road would not end until the last piece of a biblical nightmare was lived and put into place. I tried to mask regret from the driver, but I am sure he knew, and probably thought unlucky guy.

After paying the driver, I stumbled my way into the motel room and slouched upon an only chair, card in hand, starring stony faced at the words and puzzle piece, while also replaying how I came to get a business card at the Regatta. And I couldn't help but compare how an educated woman provided a business card, but reveals it doesn't show her proper employment position. In contrast however, an educated man working for an ugly bank provides his business card, but secretly avoids disclosing that it does not reflect his proper employment position. "How is it possible for déjà vu to spill into reality?" I thought to myself.

Consider the mathematical possibilities. At the very least there are several million individuals in Australia who would have business cards. What are the chances of two individuals providing their cards with incorrect details, but similar in nature; to the same person when they first meet? Further, the individuals are also poles apart, for one is at the western perimeter a country, whilst the other is at its eastern perimeter.

Indeed, what I had real difficulty with was the circumstances because both times I was in the processing of purchasing a restaurant bar, and the people with the cards had indicated a desire to help. Although, as it turned out one of those seemingly did not know what the word help meant. Nonetheless, even if you were writing a story the chances of you thinking of this particular plot would be slim. Sleep did not come easy that night, but I made a mental note to send someone flowers the next day before closing my eyes.

In the morning, after leaving the florist, I made my way back to my apartment on the Gold Coast, whilst contemplating where to next. The restaurant that I had intended to buy, also meant I would have to move to Brisbane. It wasn't a problem rather, more annoying than anything else because who likes packing? By this stage, I decided that I would continue with the flow because being the mouse type, an inquisitive mind said to follow the trail and see where it leads.

This meant responding to a message on my phone from the pretty woman I had left at the Regatta. Obviously, she must have the flowers I mused as I was writing her numbers on my scribble pad. And true enough, she liked them therefore, the next week we spent a considerable amount of time talking to each other. I did feel a little guilty because her reasons for contact were not the same as mine, but it had to be done and I really couldn't tell her why, so I carried on regardless. She was attractive and had a nice personality however, she was also a lot younger than me.

Anyway, the end result was I had to be in Brisbane the following Friday as part of the due diligence process, so I made plans to meet up with a fine young lady at the Regatta. However, later on during the week I also managed to bring a pretty woman back down to earth by mentioning my daughter and how close they were in age, less than ten years, which did shock the would be romantic. Thus, a seed of doubt had been planted, my part was to make it grow, and successful I was.

After consuming an ordinary meal at my soon to be restaurant, I met up with the pretty lady at the Regatta later on. And true to form and planning, she confirmed that her enthusiasm had waned so perhaps it was better if we were friends instead. Then as if she had been around since the beginning of time, she also commented she had never connected with someone so quickly, and still wanted me to call her? Friends, and still wanted me to call her? My experience of this scene is the woman is actually saying she wants more time because a house, white picket fence, and two children was still on her mind. Of course, I said no thanks and left the unprofessional at the Regatta.

Over the next two weeks, I did all of the necessary tasks required in relation to the sale contract. The only thing left to do was wait, so I amused myself by looking for a new place to live. But as I was driving around Brisbane, looking at potential suburbs to reside in that were close to the restaurant I became hungry. Therefore, I stopped at what I thought was a side street and parked my car adjacent to a shopping centre, because I had noticed a number of cafes one could choose to get breakfast.

The place I chose was called the Bulimba Bean Café. I sat down and then ordered what I wanted after being attended to by waiting staff. Being that the area was new to me, I surveyed the other coffee shops and businesses dotted along the small street when I noticed a familiar face, sitting with what appeared to be friends and family at the café diagonally across the road. It seemed whilst a lady had made it out of a Regatta intact, in this instance I became shipwrecked by the unexpected and hence, couldn't wait to be rescued by my meal so I could eat and sail out of there.

There is nothing worse than being haunted by a business card I am sure, especially when it has long legs, blonde hair, an angelic face, and dynamite body. Although being a human business card, the angel didn't have wings. To this day, I cannot remember when I have eaten a meal or drank a coffee faster than I did at the Bulimba Bean Café. It was similar to an eating contest, two bites, one slurp, then including yours truly everything was gone.

Another week passed by with no surprises, but the silence was annoying because I was waiting on approval from the landlord for the lease, and a green light from Liquor Licensing so I could actually settle on the sale contract. And my conscience was driving me crazy with a silly notion that I was attempting to dismiss and forget about with no guilt whatsoever. But the sounds of Judas coins jiggling in a leather bag kept piercing my dreams, ensuring a restful sleep was almost impossible.

It was almost three weeks after first meeting a lady at the Regatta, and as I was attending to a few financial forecasts at my desk the fax started whirring. The letter was an approval from the landlord of the building that housed the restaurant however, it also included a proposed new clause. As it turned out, the current owners of the restaurant were in excess of three months arrears in their rent, and because the way the lease was structured the landlord had no confidence that they would be able to guarantee my lease payments. Therefore, he agreed to the lease assignment, but he wanted a bank guarantee of three month's rent in case I had difficulty in the future.

I really didn't care about the new clause in the lease however, I was incensed that this information wasn't supplied during the due diligence process. Yes I know, the same song is becoming a bit tedious, right? Yet here it was again, because the price I was prepared to pay for the restaurant was fifty thousand dollars total, and the rental arrears of the business was equal to the purchase price. However, if I supplied the bank guarantee to satisfy the new clause in the lease I would have had to tie up another fifty thousand dollars of capital thereby, making the real purchase price double to that of my original budget and business plan.

And yes, I had every intention of teaching a Chartered Accounting Firm lessons in the Federal Court of Australia, but I required about a hundred thousand dollars or thereabouts to fund the fees for legal representation. Thus, if I provided the guarantee I wouldn't be able to hire the right law firm to win a case. Competent, professional law firms are expensive, and winning was my priority, but the incentive to pay double for a worthless business is non-existence in any case, be it if one is swimming in cash or otherwise. By this stage I can assure you that I was sick of the fibbers in my life.

Then suddenly the phone rang. It was the proprietor of 29 High Restaurant asking if I received a fax approving the lease assignment. Gritting my teeth and counting to ten so as to prevent verbal abuse, I decided to ask a few important questions about settlement because she was keen for me to take over on lease approval.

However, before I could discuss the proposed new clause in the lease, which would have meant changing a sale contract, she interrupted and informed that she would not be keeping the restaurant's doors open past Sunday. And at this stage it was eleven days before settlement was due, Liquor Licensing still had not approved the transfer, and essential services required to operate the actual business were due to commence on settlement day; not before. They included such things as the eftpos machine, phone, electricity, and so on. Therefore, I couldn't take over the business anyway, and this was not considering the statutory risk associated with selling alcohol without a liquor licence. A fine of thirty thousand dollars first offence thank you very much!

Therefore, I asked the woman on the end of a phone if she could fax a copy of her cancellation notices concerning the essential services, including the details of the bank who owned the eftpos machine. Thinking that I was being nice and wanting to take over the business she agreed, and about an hour later I received the information I had asked for. The bank details were interesting to say the least, because you wouldn't believe it, but an ugly national elephant bank with a star as its logo was her business banking partner. So in response, I picked up a business card and then did two things.

First, I wrote a letter and faxed it to the broker for the restaurant, cancelling a sale contract. Secondly, I made my way downstairs, out of the building, and headed to the local florist shop, for I planned to send the biggest bouquet of roses to a business card that was humanely possible, without destroying my budget completely of course. My temper had finally hit boiling point, and there was no return therefore, I didn't care for ramifications because a mouse had become completely fed up! Nonetheless, I did feel a little better after I had finished since my frustrations were satisfied somewhat.

Meanwhile, not simultaneously but at a similar time, Australia's Prime Minister made an address to the nation concerning his decision to support the United States determination to invade Iraq. There had been reports in the media about the dubious reasons put forward for an invasion. And queries were made concerning Mr Howard ignoring the royal prerogative, which had traditionally been the primary instrument to engage Australian troops for war.

Instead, the Governor-General and Executive were not consulted, and the Minister for Defence relied upon the (Cth) Defence Act to engage Australian forces. The decision was controversial because those who had any idea about Iraq probably knew it had no weapons of mass destruction stockpiled anywhere.

The following are the key points to Mr Howard's speech of 20 March 2003;
Particulars:

- The Government has decided to commit Australian forces to disarm Iraq because we believe it is right, it is lawful and it's in Australia's national interests.
- We are determined to join other countries to deprive Iraq of its weapons of mass destruction, its chemical and biological weapons, which even in minute quantities are capable of causing death and destruction on a mammoth scale.
- To those in the community who may not agree with me, please vent your anger against me and towards the government. Remember that our forces are on duty in the Gulf in our name and doing their job in the best traditions of Australia's defence forces.

The Iraq Survey Group (ISG) was a fact-finding mission sent by the multinational force after the 2003 invasion of Iraq, to find the weapons of mass destruction alleged to be possessed by Iraq that had been the main reason for the invasion. Its final report, *Comprehensive Report of the Special Advisor to the Director of Central Intelligence on Iraq WMD*, (*commonly referred to as the Duelfer Report*); was submitted to Congress and the President in 2004.

It consisted of a 1400-member international team organised by the Pentagon and Central Intelligence Agency, to hunt for the alleged stockpiles of weapons of mass destruction, including chemical and biological agents, and any supporting research programs or infrastructure that could be used to develop weapons of mass destruction. The report acknowledged only small stockpiles of chemical WMDs were found, the number being inadequate to pose a militarily significant threat.

Therefore, as far as Australia's involvement was concerned, no weapons of mass destruction were found that justified the invasion, or supported the details revealed in Mr Howard's address to the nation, or his decision to ignore the royal prerogative. So in essence an opportunity arose concerning a domestic legal issue affecting Australia's Constitution Act and Constitution on 20 March 2003. That opportunity was caused by negligence from a Prime Minister however, unfortunately the High Court of Australia, parliament, and those who supposedly know the law, had the opinion that whilst there may be a constitutional question, it did not give rise to any domestic legal issues.

I did not watch all of the national address by Prime Minister Howard because even with my limited knowledge I could see that he was lying through his teeth, which sickened me quite frankly. And I also couldn't care if he read this book an attempted some sort of claim concerning defamation because firstly, he would lose his case and secondly, in my view the man is a cowardly murderer. He reminds me of a snake in the garden of good and evil, slithering and slinking with dastardly intentions. Yet the US President labelled him 'the man of steel,' what a load of poppycock; Tin Man more likely, only this version had no heart and no brains!

Sadly, I did see the pictures of Australian troops saying goodbye to their loved ones as they were going to fight another overseas war, started by someone other than their country. And distressingly, their efforts had nothing to do with the notion of defending God, Crown, and country, because a negligent Prime Minister scuttled that avenue. I thought of the ANZACS and how they must have been turning in their graves at yet another dumb Prime Minister sending Australian forces to fight for a lost cause.

Moreover, seeing as I knew there was an actual domestic issue from a decision by an errant Prime Minister, that was both blasphemous and unconstitutional; my future became one of rectifying the problem without anyone knowing until I could gather the right evidence to establish my assumptions. This meant I had to make a decision that reared the haunting sound of those Judas coins jiggling in a leather bag. But a problem was if I was going to proceed it meant losing everything and everyone. Thus, it was going to be a life of disguise where those around you question your mind.

However, the reality was I been through it before therefore, going where angels fear to tread wasn't so scary anymore. I took the attitude of walking on the moon because I felt if I do not do something then Armstrong's giant leap for mankind meant nothing, and Martin Luthor King's 'I had a dream' was exactly that, an unfulfilled vision of wanting real peace for all. My view was the West is better than this, because democracy does not make war for lies, otherwise why did He die on a cross for us? No, you do not destroy His sacrifice and name; not whilst I am alive anyway.

So it was going to be similar to a Disneyland cartoon, where a mouse is walking along a chosen path in the concrete jungle when a clumsy and intellectually challenged elephant squashes him. Although, fortunately Walt was watching therefore, He drew the ending for an elephant, then resurrected the mouse so he could continue along the real path that would lead him and his country to salvation.

The Judge with a Ladder

Nothing is more barbarous than war. Nothing is more
cruel... Nothing is more pitiful than a nation being swept
along by fools.
—Daisaku Ikeda

FATE IS SOMETHING THAT SEEMS TO AFFECT many of us. You know, it's the story about if I did not have to stop and change a flat, I would have been one of those caught up in a freeway disaster. Unfortunately, when explaining strange events or things that happen, which can only be put down as fate, the educated among us always seem to disagree. Generally, most say having a flat that saves your life or prevents you from taking a doomed flight is chance, luck, fluke, and so on. Nevertheless, I say what do we call it when coincidences or chances appear in abundance concerning the same subject matter?

What I am explaining is, how do we understand our situation when the number of coincidences add up to a point where the circumstances you are caught up in can only be fate? Consider my situation, by March 2003, the amount of strangeness attached to the saga with a bank became so overwhelming that the evidence demanded a review of everything. And the worst part was I couldn't escape it therefore, I had no choice other than to embrace it. Briefly, the following explains;

- 8 January 1999 – the bank saga began on a king's birthday (Elvis Presley). And whilst it's understandable to say Presley wasn't traditional royalty, he was the King of Rock, and a coincidence can be metaphorical.

- 16 August 2001 – negotiations with the bank began on the anniversary of a king's death (Elvis Presley).
- The meeting came about after I had sent two letters to the bank's CEO. One of those letters talked about why elephants are scared of mice.
- During the meeting it was revealed bank staffs were flying kites without permission. And it was those kites, which caused the dramas.
- The bank employed seconded agents in its credit department, whose aim was to assist the kite flying by disguising transactions and identities.
- Part of the disguise used by the bank agents were false business cards.
- The bank servants involved were called Ripp and Hallet (Rip and Hell it).
- During the time I was in Western Australia meeting with bank officials, friends stayed at my apartment on the Gold Coast in Queensland. As a thankyou gift they left a drawing of a woman on my dining table.
- 11 September 2001 – two elephant type kites were flown into the World Trade Centre in New York. Allah was the inspiration.
- Easter Thursday 2002, I met a woman working at Melbas on the Gold Coast whose features replicated the picture hanging in my apartment. The artist who drew the picture had never met the woman at Melbas.
- After meeting the woman at Melbas, she sent a text message asking if I was her salvation9, which means are you my judge in biblical terms. The woman claimed she was asleep and never sent the text message, despite it being recorded on her phone.
- 12 October 2002, Bali bombings occurred in the tourist district of Kuta.
- December 2002, a deed of settlement is executed with the bank.
- 28 February 2003, at the Regatta Hotel in Toowong Brisbane, I received a business card from a woman who advised the employment details on the card are incorrect. The card had the words Job Access on it, and a picture of a green jigsaw puzzle piece as its logo.
- Receiving a business card at the Regatta replicates the nature of receiving a business card from the bank's agent. Both times were at first meetings, and the true employment details on both cards are incorrect.
- Meeting the woman and bank agent replicated the same circumstances in my business life. But at different times and different States in Australia.

Have you ever heard of the expression, if it looks like a fish, has scales like a fish, and smells like a fish, then it must be a fish? It cannot be anything else can it? So, if the coincidences are too numerous to ignore, the subject matter is about ethics, and the problem involves politics and religion, then the cause must be God yeah, because who else could it be? Surely, even the universe in all its wonder could not organise a script such as this one, so the hands of fate must be connected to a real God that even science cannot dismiss.

And this is what I was faced with after reviewing my situation from 08 January 1999 until 31 March 2003. However, what I also ascertained was another comparison that appeared to leap from my review, which led to a question of where was God in relation to the bank saga, 9/11, and invasion of Iraq?

That metaphorical comparison said; through martyrdom agents of God caused two towers to fall down. In my case, God was sitting in the middle of the bank's trading name because his blessing is part of Australia. So agents of the bank or through the word Australia; agents of God's blessing caused two taverns to fall down. Therefore, the nature of both events being bank servants flying kites and 9/11 were the same.

Further, because the agents of God in Australia unlawfully caused the taverns to fall down likewise, the metaphorical equivalent was the 9/11 agents of Allah unlawfully caused two towers to fall down in New York. And since both events were in commercial areas of two different countries and cities, they also spiritually replicated each other.

Therefore, on the face of it, my review established that Allah, or Almighty God in English; did not sanction the martyrdoms of 9/11. The problem for me however, was what would I have to do to prove it? I mean it's very well being able to see the answer when you are close to the event or you are actually part of it, but for others they may not see the same picture, so how was I going to prove it? Hence, my first thought was I must review Prime Minister Howard's decision concerning the invasion of Iraq, because if I found where God sits in relation to this matter, I would be able to establish the truth from Allah or God concerning the martyrdoms of 9/11.

However, what convinced me most of all to pursue this path was the business card of a woman because she reflected angelic natures in the Regatta Hotel. Aside from her beauty, the business card she carried had the words Job Access on it. And those who have read the Bible know Job is one of its Books. Thus, if an angel provides a business card with the word Job on it, God is calling for you to take a test of faith.

Nonetheless, in my case it was a little different because the text message from a woman who looked like a picture asking are me if I was her salvation9, the invasion of Iraq, and business card from an angel, meant God wanted me to take a test of His faith and truth. The test of faith concerned what road I had to travel, whilst the test of truth was to find where God sat in relation to Iraq. Therefore, sending roses to an angel from the Regatta, and cancelling the sale contract of a restaurant was the right thing to do, albeit those decisions would also cause some pain in the future.

Also, I had to follow a path that whilst familiar, it was my least preferred option because it meant losing a court case, which I had been steadily planning for two years concerning the ugly bank's wayward agents and accounting firm. Thus, I had to lodge a statement of claim in the Federal Court of Australia that had no hope of winning, but yet it would be the catalyst, which underpins a future where I win the war. So the road to success was a long and rocky one, because the ultimate outcome would not be controlled by me, as it relied on decisions made by others including the courts hence, my previous description of becoming a puppet on a string.

Therefore, I lodged a statement of claim in the Federal Court. However, included in the claim was an unedited fairytale about a mouse and elephant. This ensured that reliable evidence of my conscience or intention could be used to establish my ultimate claims and assertions about 9/11, the invasion of Iraq, and God's choice of religion. It would also reveal my judgment of God's involvement in the aforementioned, with the ultimate verdict of proving His innocence, despite that He knew of 9/11 beforehand.

Further, because there was no doubt in my mind that Mr Howard had made an unconstitutional decision concerning Iraq, my loss would also underpin a forgiveness rule where, guilt is carried by Almighty God, for they knew not what they were doing. Or in essence, I was going to commit a metaphorical martyrdom reflecting the Act of Christ by losing a very winnable court procedure and being put into bankruptcy. Thus, I would sacrifice my business life, but my faith would be rewarded because God was going to ensure He would resurrect a new life for me through the Book of Job.

Of course at this stage the problem for me was I did not know what sort of life God had planned therefore, despite the apprehension I had to trust my faith. And please believe me, on many occasions after the court proceeding I cursed the cards that I had been dealt because it was never my choice in the first place. Therefore, the test of faith meant at the very least I would be laughed at, jeered at, avoided, and thought insane.

Nevertheless, I implemented my plan and lodged a statement of claim in the Federal Court against the ugly bank and its agents Ferrier Hodgson. Amongst other things, I requested the following;

- Removal of the word Australia from the bank's trading name
- Criminal charges be brought against the bank and its agents
- Forty-five million four hundred and fifty thousand dollars compensation
- An order for a witness to provide her statement about the circumstances surrounding our meeting at the Regatta
- Permission to print and publish a book called; The Angel's Business Card

The reason for the unusual orders was aside from knowing that the court had no jurisdiction, it also meant the evidence supporting my assumptions would go from circumstantial to fact, because the future would reveal all. However, the annoying part was by losing a claim I would be made bankrupt, but I still required a statement from the witness to substantiate déjà vu caused by God. In other words, I still needed to prove that fate alone was the reason why two people met, or they met because it was destiny and therefore, their meeting was unavoidable for it was organised by God.

Ultimately, after losing a court case and being made bankrupt, an only choice for me was to continue annoying a woman until she either provided the written statement I required, or it was delivered through another method like say, the police and court if a trial was deemed necessary. And I can assure you it was not an enjoyable experience however; the fact was the woman refused to believe that I only wanted a statement from her. Unfortunately, she assumed my motive involved a relationship, but if she actually knew me, she would have understood that she was also not the first beautiful woman I have told to find someone else. I guess even women have egos.

So the end result was I was arrested for stalking, but I didn't care because at the same time a trial would also mean a constitutional challenge. By his stage it was mid-2004, and I probably had enough evidence to establish my assumptions, but what I did not factor was how dumb Crown lawyers were. Their actions cost three years of my life therefore, I have kept their names because they are in for a shock. Briefly, what happened was at the directions hearing before trial, I applied for the procedure to be referred to the Supreme or High Court, as I had evidence to establish a constitutional infraction affecting statehood and the indissoluble union.

On the other hand, the legal representatives for the Crown wanted me to sign an agreement where the charges would be dropped and I was not to contact the witness again. Apparently no conviction would also be recorded. Obviously, I refused for I knew they could not establish guilt on the indictment and/or charges. However, it became really interesting when a judge blew her fuse because of my refusal to sign rubbish from the Crown, and insistence that the trial be moved to a higher court.

Therefore, the silly and unprofessional District Court Judge, vacated her chair and bench without making any decision and left both parties bemused by her disgraceful attempt at intimidation. What an absolute tosser she was, and the same can be said for the Queensland District Court, which obviously is made up of low intellects. Then after that debacle, the court attempted to conduct a trial without informing when a jury was going to be picked or allowing any of my supporting witnesses to appear.

So it was a mis-trial before I even attended hence, the matter was adjourned and an indictment was referred back to the Attorney-General's Department. Subsequently, the indictment was then referred to the Mental Health Court for a forensic order of insanity. And after the Court ruled in favour of the Crown, I had to obey the terms and conditions of the order. Nevertheless, again I didn't care because the law states that the accused can still elect to have a trial instead of accepting the Mental Health Court ruling. An election, however, must be made within twenty-eight days from the receipt of the written orders by the Mental Health Court.

Consequently, I obliged because this time I was going to tear the Crown and its stinking District Court of Queensland apart. However, in response the silly Attorney–General's Department withdrew the indictment so a trial could not take place because there was no lawful instrument underpinning the charges. But things got a little worse because the same idiots then carried on with the Mental Health Court's forensic order thereby, I appealed and won my case. The Court ruled in favour of my application based on my argument that if there is no indictment then the charges were void and the forensic order had no legal grounds underpinning its authority. So I say to you, seeing that I represented myself, if I was insane how could I know the law because the very essence of insanity is the person does not know what they are doing or saying.

Anyway, the upshot is I had my statement from the Regatta witness, and beat inept lawyers and judges in the process. And while there were many episodes of silliness, I ignored them and set about finishing what I started hence, the reason for this book.

Difficult Questions

I refuse to accept the view that mankind is so tragically
bound to the starless midnight of racism and war that the
bright daybreak of peace and brotherhood can never
become a reality... I believe that unarmed truth and
unconditional love will have the final word.
—Martin Luthor King, Jr.

PROBABLY THE MOST DIFFICULT SUBJECT TO WRITE OR TALK about is religion, its differences, and its fanatical followers. However, because of 9/11 and the war on terror it is a conversation that must be had. To begin with, the first question is what is the difference between a fanatical Christian and a fanatical Muslim? The answer is none because both sides have no tolerance or logical perception of true faith. If history is a confirmation of anything, true faith is defined by the famous who have been persecuted, but in their despair, they have resisted the resolution of violence. Mohandas Ghandi, Martin Luthor King Jr, and Nelson Mandela are three modern day examples of true faith.

Their faith and beliefs resonated in a determination that protest for fundamental change can happen without violence. Ghandi provided the inspiration and way for India's democratic freedom, through persecution and pacifism Mandela provided the inspiration for the dissolution of apartheid, and via his speech of 'I have a dream' King Jr provided a defining moment for the civil rights movement in the United States of America. Not one of those greats required to win a revolution by the barrel of a gun but unfortunately, one can't say the same for those involved in 9/11 or Iraq's invasion and yet, including Osama bin Laden apparently, they were educated men.

Nevertheless, what if someone did have an answer because they could actually prove what they claimed was true? And the definition of truth in this instance is from the Oxford Dictionary and not a politician's dictionary. Further, what if that truth reveals an opportunity where it can be shown that God exists, and He has chosen one to provide the solution to a festering religious problem, which appears to be getting worse as the years fly buy? Would you believe that person or would you check the facts first and upon confirmation support the claim?

As a reader, whether you are from Australia, the United States, England, or any other nation involved in the invasion of Iraq, or not for that matter, we all know that the war was based on lies. However, lies or otherwise, is it possible to prove that the decision to invade Iraq, was the right thing to do? Or alternatively, is it possible to prove that "God told President Bush to do it?" I believe it is.

I base my assumptions and conclusions on not only what has happened to me but also, a situation where an unauthorised betrayal of God in Australia's Constitution Act and Constitution occurred because of an address to the nation on 20 March 2003, by former Prime Minister Howard. The betrayal came about because firstly, Mr Howard lied about the reasons for an invasion and secondly, he ignored the Executive power or royal prerogative to gain proper permission to make war. So in reality the blessing from God that Australia humbly relies on was not considered at all, and yet the events causing Iraq's invasion namely, the 9/11 martyrdoms, came from religion.

Nevertheless, despite the cause stemming from religion whether under the name of terrorism or otherwise, Iraq's invasion actually wasn't based in religion. Therefore, the duty of Mr Howard was to get constitutional permission for making war, which he did not do. In my view, the reason he did not get permission was he knew there were no weapons of mass destruction, and had worked out that nobody would be able to hold him accountable if he ignored protocol, because those around him, including the Queen, do not know the Constitution.

And he could also count on the courts for no involvement, because as I have proven, the first action from the judges was to act like ostriches and bury their heads in sand hoping no person would notice. Of course, there was outcry from the legal fraternity and others, but the reality was no person actually did anything about it. However, if Australia had its own Head of State, I venture to say a former Prime Minister may have had a problem. But regrettably, having our own Head of State is just wishful thinking.

Anyway, the point I am making is there was a constitutional problem caused by former Prime Minister Howard that implicated Australia's indissoluble Federation or Statehood, which could have been exploited by the Islamic religion if their shepherds or leaders were awake. Fortunately they weren't. This problem could have meant that it was possible to prove Allah did sanction 9/11, and in turn, this would have provided an insurmountable inspiration for terrorists the world over to unite with far more cohesion than they have demonstrated thus far.

And it isn't hard to work out because the cries of Allah would have been ringing around the world, if Islamic leaders in Australia were awake enough to use their influence and make a media case out of the standing of Australia's Constitution Act, Constitution, indissoluble Federation, and Statehood.

The Constitutional Problem

Religion is not everyone's cup of tea
particularly for those of us who like coffee.
—Eric Spain 2018

USTRALIA HAD A CONSTITUTIONAL PROBLEM that no one appeared to notice, although speaking from experience I tend to believe the courts (judges) were aware, but they said nothing. The problem stemmed from the address to the nation on 20 March 2003, by former Prime Minister John Howard, and his decision not to use the royal prerogative when engaging Australian forces to invade Iraq. Both decisions were unconstitutional to the point where it could have easily been shown the High Court of Australia and indeed, the Crown of Australia, had no jurisdiction owing to the interaction between the preamble of the Constitution Act, and paragraph 116 of the Constitution.

And because it could have been shown that the Crown and High Court of Australia had no lawful jurisdiction from 20 March 2003, the ramifications would have been drastic to say the least. For example; when it comes to criminal law despite what a parliamentary statute says, because it could have been proven the High Court had no lawful jurisdiction since 20 March 2003, a trial conducted by the respective States and Territories of Australia, that falls under the appellate of the High Court, could have been deemed a mistrial as there would not have been a proper path to a right of appeal.

Or alternatively, since it could have been proven the High Court, via Prime Minister Howard's decision to invade Iraq, had lost its original jurisdiction to hear appeals from a State or Territory trial, any decision it would have made from 20 March 2003, could actually have been established as null and void.

This is explained in the following manner:

- The preamble of the Australian Constitution Act says; *WHEREAS the people of New South Wales, Victoria, South Australia, Queensland, and Tasmania, humbly relying on the blessing of Almighty God, have agreed to unite in one indissoluble Federal Commonwealth under the Crown of the United Kingdom of Great Britain and Ireland, and under the Constitution hereby established.*

- Moreover, Paragraph 5 of the Constitution Act says; *This Act, and all laws made by the Parliament of the Commonwealth under the Constitution, shall be binding on the courts, judges, and people of every State and of every part of the Commonwealth, notwithstanding anything in the laws of any State; and the laws of the Commonwealth shall be in force on all British ships, the Queen's ships of war excepted, whose first port of clearance and whose port of destination are in the Commonwealth.*

- Whilst paragraph 116 of the Constitution says; *The Commonwealth shall not make any law for establishing any religion, or for imposing any religious observance, or for prohibiting the free exercise of any religion, and no religious test shall be required as a qualification for any office or public trust under the Commonwealth.*

Therefore, an interaction between the preamble and paragraph 116 is clear as it confirms the Commonwealth cannot change the status quo or traditional laws, which govern the indissoluble Federation or union. A reason is due to the phrase 'relying on God's blessing'. Thus, the word *relying* is gerund or ongoing until such time as another arrangement is made, whilst in comparison a word such as *relied* on is a past tense scenario because it has ended at some point. Hence, to this day as far as constitutional law is concerned, the entire indissolubility of the Federation is wholly and solely still relying on God's blessing. If that blessing is desecrated then likewise, so is the union.

Ultimately, the previous means when the interaction between the preamble and paragraph 116 is considered, the Commonwealth cannot make any law, change, or impose an observance by physical or wordless implication, which is inconsistent with the traditional Law or Word of God. And since the blessing is by Almighty God, those traditional laws are the Ten Commandments, for they are the only known laws written and canonized by Him.

Or alternatively, Australia's continued reliance on God's blessing for its indissoluble Federation is governed by the Ten Commandments for they are written, and not an unreliable verbal arrangement that can be devolved from time to time. So when Prime Minister Howard lied about weapons of mass destruction in his address to the nation on 20 March 2003, and also, ignored the royal prerogative to engage Australian forces for an invasion based on those lies, in effect he contravened the rules governing the indissoluble Federation thereby, making it dissoluble without the need for a referendum.

Further, he also contravened paragraph 116 of the Constitution because the action has forced an observance, which has not only changed the Commandments, but also the result has devolved God's blessing concerning the indissoluble union without authorisation. Or Mr Howard's decisions have devalued or rescinded Federation's reliance on God for its indissolubility.

Moreover, since it can also be proven that the Crown, High Court, parliament, and government have tacitly allowed the devaluation of God's blessing by Mr Howard, then the entire Commonwealth is in contravention of paragraph 116 of the Constitution as well. The contravention is clear because the Commonwealth has no authority to devolve the rules that govern the indissolubility of Federation, as this right belongs in the hands of the people by referendum.

Thus, the Commonwealth is tacitly or wordlessly forcing a religious observance over the people, which reflects that either God is a statue or the Federation no longer relies upon God's blessing for its indissolubility. And since the Commonwealth's insinuation is untrue, unlawful, and unconstitutional, it means both Crown and High Court of Australia have no jurisdiction, because in effect there is no reliable blessing to keep the indissoluble Federation within its original composition.

Or the Federal Commonwealth is unconstitutional, so its authorities or courts have no lawful grounds to underpin enforcement of statutes, including criminal; passed by its parliament. Thus, Australia's Constitution Act and Constitution are useless law instruments because they no longer have reliable authority, as it can be proven their composition can be adjusted or devolved without the need for a referendum.

And the cause creating the illegality against the Commonwealth is Commandment 9, which states; "thou shall not lie," because now it appears the Commandment says; "thou can lie if you are a Prime Minister and want to make war for any reason."

Thus, the Commonwealth as a whole is in contravention of the rules that are used to make God's blessing reliable, which in turn keep the Federation in its original form of indissolubility. Or in a nutshell, no lawful Constitution Act, then no legitimate High Court, and no right to an official path of appeal under a lawful Constitution.

Moreover, paragraph 116 of the Constitution actually relies upon God's blessing to be a lawful statute under the indissoluble Federation. So the only definition for God's blessing is the Ten Commandments. And supporting the blessing's meaning is part of their structure has been adopted by Australia in legislated laws concerning criminal violations such as stealing and murder.

Therefore, the blessing from God for the indissoluble Federal Commonwealth can only be constitutional and must be based upon His written Commands. Otherwise the blessing would, in fact and law, be a religious observance where His reliability can change from time to time, depending on new theology or interpretations by members of parliament, or other authorities of the Commonwealth.

Nonetheless, the more damming aspect of what could have happened concerns the opportunity surrounding Australia's Head of State (Queen of England). By being able to dissolve the indissoluble Federation without the need for a referendum would have meant abdication for a Queen. Further, it also would have meant that 9/11 could have been proven to be sanctioned by Allah (Almighty God) because a Prime Minister lied thereby, desecrating the indissoluble union's holy blessing. Or God favours Al Qaeda because they did not lie about 9/11, whilst a Prime Minister lied about Iraq.

This may have been embarrassing for Christianity and democracy to say the least, as the fallout would have meant, via 9/11 Allah or Almighty God was punishing the wicked in the west for their decadence and so on. And again the actions of a Muslim proving the facts in a High Court of Australia may have provided an insurmountable inspiration for an almost unstoppable terrorist force. Or it may have meant millions of martyrs being set loose upon the world with devastating consequences, because they would have proof Al Qaeda was right. Imagine the martyrs Al Qaeda could have recruited after a court case in Australia.

Luckily it did not happen, because someone was watching and therefore, interfered in my life to the point where my attention was captured. That someone of course was God and His interference in my case against a bank and its wayward agents. The small clue, however, came from a business card with the words Job Access printed on it.

The Cost of a Sacrifice

Australia is a democratic pearl;
the ANZACS are its protecting oyster.
—Eric Spain 2018

WHAT WOULD YOU DO? AS A NORMAL CITIZEN what would you do if you were in say, the same boat as me at the time of former Prime Minister Howard's address to the nation, and you knew it would open a loophole in your nation's Constitution, where there is a possible domestic threat to Federation or Statehood? Further, what if that threat actually came from a Godlike scenario where the result meant that just one person could dissolve the indissoluble? But in order to secure the indissolubility the result also meant that you had to lose everything.

What do you think your decision would have been, and be honest because it is far easier to make judgement after the event? As I have stated earlier, this was the choice I had to make in 2003. I could see the loophole and the only way to close it was by a sacrifice of some sort because the action meant preventing evil from arising. And let's face it when it comes to God and Lucifer, surprise is their 'modus operandi,' with the prime example being 9/11 of course.

Therefore, say you are walking in my shoes and the choice is in front of you, but the combatants are spiritual in physicality and nature. How would you prevent that spirit from achieving its objective because all you have is the Act of Christ to thwart hope of victory for an evil assassin? Would you sacrifice everything to save everyone or would you ignore the threat and take say, a pile of the money instead? As I have already explained, my decision was to be the sacrificial lamb and do what I believed was right, rather than win a claim against a wayward bank and its agents.

I did so for many reasons, but most of all because a long time ago others much braver than me faced a real sacrifice for their country. And it is their legend that I was born and raised under because they fought for God, King, and country foremost. Oh, I have no doubt that like me they did not want to take the path they had to, but in reality they had no choice because God, King, and country meant everything to them.

These are Prime Minister Howard's words not mine;

- To those in the community who may not agree with me, please vent your anger against me and towards the government. Remember that our forces are on duty in the Gulf in our name and doing their job in the best traditions of Australia's defence forces.

Our forces are on duty in the Gulf in our name and doing their job in the best traditions of Australia's defence forces? Excuse me for asking, but if a Prime Minister tells lies and ignores the royal prerogative, how were Australian forces representing God, Crown, and country in the tradition of the ANZACs? Where is the symbolisation for 25 April? How is it possible to be in the best traditions of the ANZACS in 1915, if the invading forces in Iraq were there because of lies and no other constitutional or traditional reason whatsoever?

No God, no Crown, and no country only lies from a former Prime Minister, who sided with the United States and England to invade the weakest country in the Middle East. This was my scenario because how was it possible for a soldier's soul to be saved if they had no official approval from Almighty God to take a life in Iraq? Were the armed forces at fault? Of course not because they have a duty to obey orders, so they cannot question the soundness of a decision by a Prime Minister or President for that matter. Nevertheless, the problem was no God, no Crown, and no country.

The fact of the matter is, Australia's indissoluble Federation relies on the blessing of God and not the Queen or Crown of England. Therefore, if a Prime Minister ignores the royal prerogative to make war there is no constitutional basis on which to underpin the decision particularly, when it involves lies in the first instance.

And it is easy to work out because the term 'royal' belongs to God and the Crown, not a Prime Minister. So if there isn't royalty involved in the decision under the terms of Australia's Federation, it's impossible to be officially representing the country, so how in the world was Mr Howard's decision lawful in any way whatsoever?

So for me the reality was to forego all of my plans and put the country first because I could see a problem that would have turned into a nightmare if I ignored the obvious. And the nightmare was real because it would have meant that through the lies of Iraq the terrorists had an opportunity to prove Allah sanctioned 9/11. Therefore, it came down to a spiritual prevention rather than anything else. That is before evil had time to counter against a Prime Minister's decision, I sacrificed my business life before it was officially confirmed that Iraq had no weapons of mass destruction.

Thus, forgiveness for everyone dear Almighty God, which under the terms of a sacrifice meant that no evil could arise through Australia's Federation or Statehood. An only problem for me was, however, it meant a President, two Prime Ministers, and British Crown were also forgiven even though they did not deserve it. Which obviously brings me back to the point of proving the United States President said, "God told him to do it," because owing to a sacrifice, in effect those words are true.

Nevertheless, despite preventing evil from rising in a Federation and Constitution in 2003, another problem for me was those numbers sent in three text messages by a woman I had met in Easter of 2002. As I have explained, those text messages started with *are you my salvation9*, and together the numbers meant 9172533. To me, before I decided to sacrifice a business life, dismissing the number 9; I did not know if the Job Access business card from an angel in the Regatta meant one or seventeen years in the wilderness where, no friends, no family, and no life would be part of the deal.

I also assumed the other numbers meant something else in the future and I was right, because seventeen years later I am writing the last piece of a puzzle where, once published, I am a free man to do what I want again without interference from God. And I can assure you that those seventeen years haven't been a pleasant experience, so I am glad it's over. During this time, aside from a small respite in 2007, where after the debacle with the Queensland courts and Attorney-General's Department between the years 2004-07, I thought my job had been completed; I was able to see the one I love most on this planet.

The person who am referring to is my daughter. The reality is, during the last seventeen years I have only spent one Christmas with her. I have missed all of her birthdays from when she turned sixteen onwards. I have missed her engagement, her wedding, and never seen my grandchildren. She once told me that I had broken her heart and after saying so has never spoken to me again.

As a parent, the worst words you can ever hear from your child are you have broken their heart because it means a severance of true love. That is no trust and no belief of what you once stood up for because to them it was lies in the beginning, so you have never loved them from the start. And the absolute worst part is, because of the lies from religion and politics, as well as the circumstances surrounding the Book of Job, you cannot explain why you have changed, and you are sorry for breaking their heart.

Am I sorry that I broke her heart, absolutely. However, if you refer to the Book of Job you will find that all of his sons and daughters were killed by evil therefore, in my defence because of a business card, I distanced myself from everyone. Then I pointed out to God under all things religion those innocents around me could not be harmed, as constitutional forgiveness for a Prime Minister's lies had been affected in 2003. It didn't mean that I could escape seventeen years of torment, but it did allow a beautiful daughter to have the life she wanted, albeit without me.

Fortunately, for me, this saga has ended. And whilst this is only a short story, there are other longer versions with different endings and possible consequences. I have published all them on Amazon.com, but do not really care if they sell or otherwise, as the potential domestic issue of Australia losing its Federation to evil was thwarted in 2003. Therefore, restoration of the sacrifice those ANZACS made was achieved, and as time has proven, no evil or domestic threat has arisen in Australia. But I deserve no credit because in reality it was Almighty God who saved Australia. However, He did so because of His affection for those brave forces in 2015, where a nation was truly born in their sacrifice for God, King, and country.

Nevertheless, perhaps the dumbest constitutional body of the indissoluble union is the High Court of Australia. If a union solely relies upon God for its indissolubility, but that reliance is desecrated, how is it possible for an administrative body formed under its instrumentation or paragraphs able to maintain its authorisation?

Or alternatively, how is it possible for the High Court not to know or understand who Australia relies on for its authorisation? Australia does not rely on its Queen for authorisation rather, the Crown relies upon God's blessing for the indissoluble Federal Commonwealth to be formed under its authority otherwise, there is actually no Crown of Australia. This shows that not only are the High Court judges dumb, but also every other judge in Australia is likewise, because they don't know how the Constitution Act works or how Federation maintains its indissolubility.

The Angels Business Card

Book One
(Short Version)

P. S. ... Through New York Eyes

EAR READER ... NOW THAT I HAVE YOUR ATTENTION, whilst the path you are on includes God it is based from a Mouse type perspective. So basically, there are two reasons for telling this story. Firstly, Almighty God; and secondly, whilst religious testimonies appear to be fairytales, it also seems that due to our historical education those encounters may actually be true.

Therefore, rather than the usual religious reasons of death and destruction perhaps we should consider another perspective along the lines of if He does exist, then what is His opinion in relation to all things of Jumbo importance? And if He doesn't exist, how can we use a silent voice to prove what His opinion may entail? Of course, before beginning maybe it's also wise to reveal the inspiration that led me to find answers for these seemingly impossible questions.

Perhaps this story really began on 03 August 2001, in a fax to the National Australia Bank, which talked about an old book and its history. Anyway, years later after the CEO and his Roman type bank didn't keep its word, in answer to my plea that Romeo should remove Australia from its trading name, I received a reply from the Chairman.

This was because bank agents, who created the problems, played unethical games causing bankruptcy and the loss of family and friends. Part of my letter included the fax of 01, which said; finally Frank, have you read The Art of War? I think you should send a copy to Mr. Jacobs because it explains why Elephants are scared of Mice, particularly Mice who have the ability to think.

The fax forms part of a Deed of Settlement with the bank, but its reference to Mr. Jacobs was in relation to accountants being outsourced in its asset structuring department, who secretly worked for private firms simultaneously and passed credit files onto their bosses; some of them had the same clients as the bank.

Anyway, one night in a hotel called the Regatta whilst thinking about how to rescue a country from the Elephant bank, I was pondering how a Mouse may solve problems when a woman interrupted my thoughts with "never stand in the way of a girl trying to get to a bar." Then she introduced herself as a single girl with a mortgage. So being a person who doesn't like missing opportunities, one thing led to another until she wanted me to keep a business card, which despite its details being the same wasn't quite right because the card's job description didn't show her true position.

And because I was linked to a deed with bank fairytales printed on business cards, there was an overwhelming sense of déjà vu. At the time, I thought what are the chances of history repeating itself immediately after the first incident? But upon thinking about it, I decided to send flowers.

However, when deciding on what bouquet to send the florist created a surprise because she said, "A woman must be an angel to deserve such a generous sized bunch of roses." But my response appeared bemusing because the lady wasn't a friend and we were going separate ways. Subsequently, it created another question because the florist asked, "Why send flowers?" So, in an effort to solve confusion I gave her my business card and stood in silence as she read the words on its back, which said:

This is for them because they were only boys dressed as men, who ended as ghosts to haunt Australia's mind.

Curiously, the florist frowned for a moment, walked to the front door and changed the store sign from open to close. Next, but without urgency, she took a chair from near the doorway leading to an office and, before sitting down, placed it at the end of the counter. Then a faint, almost knowing smile formed at the corners of her lips, as she flipped through the pages and read about all things roses and thorns in ...

The Dumbo Precedent

Brought to you by the King of Spades and the Mice who rocked Romeo and His Gang

An Interview About Roman Plates

FLORIST: "WHO IS CLIKY MOUSE?"

Storyteller: "Angel Lawyer; Number 91725333 recurring or J. D. J's business card."

Florist: "So why should anyone believe what a Mouse has to say?"

Storyteller: "Whether anyone believes a Mouse is their choice. Once upon a time there was Mickey Mouse in a cartoon somewhere, but it didn't take long for humans to believe him."

Florist: "Ok, for the exercise, why is Cliky here?"

Storyteller: "Imagine if you were an ordinary person going about your life and for no reasons, apart from God, events that can't be explained seemed to repeat themselves. And we aren't talking about the movies because these circumstances are based on fact, but perhaps a way to maintain sanity is to pretend one is in a fairytale."

Florist: "How do you mean?"

Storyteller: "A few years ago an event occurred where an Elephant type bank was caught being naughty. So as a result of negotiations a man entered into a contract, but after settlement the Elephant misbehaved again. Anyway, throughout the next fourteen months or so various other settlements occurred until finally one last deed was agreed with, but in doing so the bank and its E-OR gang were warned that if they didn't stop, war would be next."

Florist: "Dare we say that it happened again?"

Storyteller: "Yes and no."

Florist: "What do you mean?"

Storyteller: "Well, this time round the person thought it may have a lot to do with two business cards, therefore reinforcements were required."

Florist: "So it wasn't the Elephant's fault?"

Storyteller: "No, it was the bank's fault because its gang started the problems, but somehow a woman's business card and mortgage also become stuck in the sand with the Dumbos."

Florist: "And a Mouse was called in to fix the situation because everyone knows women and Elephants are scared of Mice; right?"

Storyteller: "So you have seen Walt's cartoons. Anyway, that's roughly what happened, a lady left her business card and then an Australian was in Disneyland."

Florist: "Ok, so how did the saga begin?"

Storyteller: "A man was in a regatta when he crossed a lady's path and for reasons he finds difficult to believe, he was at the beginning again."

Florist: "What sort of Mouse is Cliky and where does he live?"

Storyteller: "He connects with all computers and hangs ten in lost E-mail land."

Florist: "What do the initials J D J mean?"

Storyteller: "Jack Daniel Jersusa."

Florist: "And what do Mice do in lost E-mail land?"

Storyteller: "Tie leashes on Elephant kites and pin their kinky tales."

Florist: "How old is Cliky?"

Storyteller: "Cliky was borne from an Angel's Business Card, so his age is a-BC."

Florist: "Why use the Hollywood stars with furry tails?"

Storyteller: "Because Dumbos fly in fairytales with stars from Disneyland such as Winnie and Eeyore. But the difference with life is, if Dumbo tales fly with Sesame Street stories they crash since Jackasses add steel blades to ivory towers, which causes the decimal points to lose their eerie wings. In other words, the glass won't hold so a Jumbo's trunk is parmesan, but unlike cheese the smell isn't honey because it's a rose garden instead."

Florist: "What does 91725333 recurring stand for?"

Storyteller: "Are you God's salvation nine? Yes, the number one knows that. Will a Mouse be prepared to honour and obey His commands from number seven? Of course because Cliky knows that's the Almighty's number two. Okay, what happens when the Mouse gets to number five? Well Cliky can't get past His favourite Son, so can we please maintain the recurring three because there isn't any tolerance on the number six, or rosy tales with decimal points."

The Players

ALMIGHTY GOD: THE GRACEFUL ACE (Walt or the real Ace of Spades)

Lucifer: *Luci (Miss Daisy with the Warner Bros Stars)*

Cliky Mouse: *Romeo's Nemesis (Joker with Slingshots)*

Pashen Miner: *Flower in a Tower (Mary's Mouse)*

The Other Mouse: *The Twin's Enemy (Thief with a Sword)*

J D Jersusa: *The Persecuted Australian (with New York Eyes)*

Single Girl with a Mortgage: *Princess in a Regatta (Puzzling Card)*

Burymore: *Jack's Corporation (Invisible Hands for Their Sad Days)*

The Man of Steel: *Barabbas (Tin Man Flying with Alice in Australia)*

E Bar and Liar's Saloon: *Wall Street (Two Towers)*

Mary Street Nightclub / 29 High St Restaurant: *Bali (Dumbo Cards)*

Hope Valley: *The Middle East (Wildcard Territory)*

Romeo: *Elephant with Stars (Kinky Tale with Broken Stories)*

Romeo's Twin: *IRAQ (another Kinky Tale with Broken Stories)*

Fairysons Chartered Accountants: *Skeleton Trunk (Unholy Deeds)*

Mr Jacobs: *see Marty (the Skeleton's Spade)*

Mr Jones: *refer to Bobby (the Skeleton's Handle)*

Mr Lorry: *Winnie (Not the Real One!)*

Jaques Lawyers: *see Fairysons (Euro Disney with Loony Toons)*

Geewatahouse Coopers Accountants: *Romeo's Agents (with Rose Glasses)*

Mr Ripp and Mr Hallet: *Flying Jumbo Kites (Pilates with Tales)*

Elmer: *Driving Miss Daisy in a Merry Car (Washington's Circus Act)*

Judiciary: *Preachers and Pilate Hands (Laundry Department)*

Other Features: *Politicians in Prayer (Carrots in a loose Bunch)*

Storyteller: *Donkey Two Tales (Persecuted Australian in Disguise)*

The Story So Far

(Their Fairytale Beginning but a Nightmare in the End)

O N 08 JANUARY 1999, IN BUNBURY WESTERN AUSTRALIA; the directors from a firm called MGY Accounting decided to purchase another Practice. Unfortunately, unbeknown to them the business appeared to have liabilities that weren't disclosed by the outgoing principal or financier for all parties namely; the National Australia Bank. Then after settlement the former owner was made bankrupt, but despite dishonouring cheques regularly the bank denied knowledge. Therefore, to fund underserved losses and costs with a buyout, MGY's Manager Jack Jersusa moved to the city of Perth in search of new business.

Eventually, a land opportunity arose that seemed to provide a full recovery, but shortly after approval the manager responsible for a proposed new loan resigned, so things were referred to the credit department. Consequently, in March 2001 at a meeting with the bank's credit officer Bob Jacobs, a business card was provided that advertised he was a bank employee when in fact he wasn't. Next, after appointing his real boss Martin Jones as the financial investigator into the affairs of Jersusa's company (Burymore), and threatening to squash him like a bug, the officer insisted a related firm that owned two taverns needed to be put into administration.

This meant a promised bank loan was revoked, which cancelled Jersusa's plans and created more losses. Nevertheless, because a bank had his cheque book, land, and taverns, in July 2001 he realised only a miracle could save him, so Jack gave up arguing and left WA. And upon arriving in Queensland all he had was ten thousand dollars, two books called Thick Face Black Heart and The Art of War, music from a rock band known as U2, and a fair degree of faith.

So in an effort to get his assets back and calm stormy waters, he wrote to the bank's CEO, but in the form of a squashed Mouse. In other words, the letters in question weren't perfect because he only wrote them once, so comprehension wasn't a strict rule, plus forgiveness was left out altogether. However, there was a method to the plan, which included editing the letters into a story and referring the contents to God and many others. That way his efforts might gain some attention.

Besides, in Jack's mind the only difficulty was finding God because it seemed a world had lost His address. Thereby, his idea was to send evidence of sliced tales or fallen stories everywhere via the distress signals method, and that way God's attention would be gained somehow. Still not much of a plan if you think about it, but the upside was if God's attention was attracted somehow, then a squashed Mouse would have a Whale of a tale on his side.

Even so, whilst it wasn't much of a plan and perhaps more of an idea really; his letters gained attention because Jack received a reply asking him to arrange a meeting with the Head of Asset Structuring for the bank in Western Australia, namely senior executive officer Lorry. The meeting disclosed several revelations such as the standard denial from the bank that it had caused wrong, or alternatively, a Dumbo type wasn't guilty of squashing any Mice.

Of course it appeared as if the Elephant had forgotten that there were contractors masquerading as employees in its credit department, and on this occasion part of the ingredients included temptation associated with land and a sudden rise in its value. The land in question was called Hope Valley and it had been rezoned from rural to industrial, thus tripling in value. But Jack thought; why would a bank with huge legal resources want a meeting unless there was information within his initial letters that proved something wasn't right?

It may have been evidence that a servant had transferred money from an unrelated account into his account to supposedly hide an unauthorised overdraft excess, or it may have been something else. He wasn't sure because after a meeting with the bank it seemed an employee wasn't alone in performing this manoeuvre. "Flying kites" is how Mr Lorry described the transfers. Although, perhaps a visionary view was the kites were Jumbo sized ones! Anyway, in December 2002, after many attempts at finding different resolutions, a final Deed of Settlement was executed between Jersusa and the bank.

The deed also disclosed the false business card affair and ethics of the bank's questionable agents. But just when it seemed he could return to having a normal life, out of the blue two incorrectly addressed letters arrived from Mr Jones blaming Jack for the demise of two taverns named in the deed. And despite the deed proving his innocence; the letters demanded thousands of dollars compensation for liquidation of the company, which owned the taverns. So because the E–ORS had gone too far this time, after replying to the agents in January 2003, Jack also thought he may have to use the Heavenly Cannons to provide Mr Jacobs and Mr Jones some Pilate lessons.

Then in February 2003, Jack was in a hotel called the Regatta when a lady interrupted his thoughts with; *never stand in the way of a girl trying to get to a bar.* But after buying the lady and her friends a drink, she told Jack that she was a single girl with a mortgage and gave him a dubious business card with the words Job Access on it. Nevertheless, although he didn't enjoy letting chances go by, on this occasion Jack sent the lady roses whilst accepting a job offer from her business card instead.

The following explains how being interrupted by a lady with a Job Access business card led to meeting a Mouse and his heavenly gang, who decided to create havoc in a man's life. They claimed they were sent to Australia by an Ace Detective called Chris Robbins, chief investigator of all things in heaven apparently. And they insisted that Jack was the one they were looking for albeit, it took another fifteen years or so for an Aussie male to reluctantly agree with what they wanted him to do.

Have You Heard the News

CE DETECTIVE CHRISTOPHER ROBBINS TURNS TO CLIKY MOUSE and asks: "The Bible says only God can give permission for Lucifer's angels to do evil deeds. So how does the Elmer hunting cartoon prove Judas was responsible for the Jumbos of 9/11, when the President said that Iraq had weapons of mass destruction, and Saddam was the Ace of Spades in the axis of evil?"

Cliky: "Because the President's claim has only revealed a three of clubs in Alice's land, and how dumb smarties are. For example; if the terrorists had referred to the Book of Revelation, Islam may have been God's preferred choice, or if the President had done the same he may have been Moses of the USA. But it seems the man of steel's x-ray vision didn't see the large print."

Chris: "Well okay, so where did you find the answer to the Jumbos of New York?"
Cliky: "When the President's imagination was flying, we decided to look for Dumbo tales in other areas, because we had just come from Sesame Street and the answer wasn't there."

Chris: "But what made you look in Australia?"
Cliky: "Well according to Elmo, the Ace of Spades was buried in Iraq, but a man of steel flew to Australia. So we looked for a DC character down under because his statue also has iron pins with eerie brackets in a frame. Next, we found Tin Man flying with Alice in Wonderland, but the Jack of Hearts was smiling because he knew an Ace of Spades was missing; so we used E-OR tales to keep the lawyers busy, whilst he played cards with the Queen. Then he trumped their tricks with an Irish Rose and the King of Spade's Thorny Crown beneath the Southern Cross, in a Sunburnt Country's Garden. So as reward His Island was given keys to their chains in an email from God. Thus, we have sent a copy around the world to a Dumbo CEO titled ..."

Hollywood Stars and Candy Stripes

DEAR MR PRESIDENT AND WASHINGTON'S CIRCUS ON CAPITAL HILL

Elmer, Winnie, Tin Man, Alice, and the Queen's Playing Cards

Do you think Elephants are scared of Mice, because included is an entertaining portrayal of how to pin tales on E-ORS. And please don't think that I have misspelt tales because the other types don't apply here. Obviously, this means that no actual animals have been hurt. Besides, when it comes to Mother Nature's tails I don't believe some Jackasses are as dumb as humans.

The following explains ...

Once there were three 'EOs' discussing how to repair problems Warner Brothers and Disneyland faced from a disaster caused by two jokers known as Bugs and Daffy; who swayed E-OR Pilates called Marty and Bobby from the wildlife theme park, and several Elephants in Dumbo's circus to take joyrides. Apparently, Dumbo had given the Jumbos His magic blessing from Walt so they could fly, but their antics meant a few stories from Sesame Street failed to stand up to scrutiny. So the result meant glass roses and kinky tales with unhappy endings were scattered everywhere.

One of the 'EOs', whose name was Elmer, wasn't happy so he enlisted Winnie (not the real one, but still smelling like pooh from daisies!), and a 'man of steel' to help fix the situation. During their meeting it was suggested the trio had no option but to open hunting season on Bugs and Daffy with their E-OR mates, for they had weapons of mass destruction and were going to ruin Wonderland's heavenly garden. This meant production would be severely hampered and there would be no carrots for Christmas. Also, Elmer had labelled Bugs and Daffy as an Ace of Spades, because he didn't know who was who and wanted them rubbed out from Disneyland contracts, "For a cwazy Wabbit with a tarred and feathered earwy Duck's shadow had gone too far this time!"

Meanwhile, upstairs in His studio high above the earth somewhere, Walt and the Angels were watching strange events unfolding down in cartoon land, but with more than just a passing interest I may add. So before Elmer and friends were implementing their respective Justice Leagues to hunt down Bugs and Daffy, instead Walt had a meeting with His Angelic followers and discussed their situation.

Apparently, the problem was Elmer, Winnie (not the real one), and the man of steel had failed to ask if they could use Walt's cards from Wonderland, and so a real Chairman wasn't happy, because He felt the Queen had betrayed His commands and exposed the hearts in His deck for no Godlike reasons.

It seemed a hunting season in the wildlife theme park could have been avoided, if only Elmer had asked Walt if he could use the Heavenly Cannons to ensure the rest of the circus would find Bugs and Daffy and bring them to justice; rather than create another disaster as they looked for jokers in wildcard territory. That way, whilst there may have been a heartbreaking mess to clean up on Sesame Street, at least casualties from the Queen's cards would be kept to a minimum.

So as a result of the meeting between Walt and His Angels, rather than fire buckshot from the ground like Elmer and his tin type helpers, Christopher Robbins was called to send his band to find where the Chairman's magic trick was. Previously, to protect Walt's Star from being hijacked, the Angels had decided to hide Heaven's Ace (the real magic) in Wonderland under Alice and Tin Man's noses. This meant that in the future Walt's starring Act wouldn't be at risk of wayward gunfire from Elmer and the rest of the hot heads from a theme park, and when the dust settled He could come forward and show His eerie but Amazing Crown again.

Therefore, because Christopher Robbins was smarter than your average character in a story, rather than send a band who were similar to Tin Man or his comedic mates to find an Ace, Mice with their slingshots were sent to protect His Ivory nails and magic, whilst Elmer and the gang set about destroying everything.

However, along the way it appears as if the Mice were blind ones and became lost searching for His eerie wings and steely points, and instead of being in Hollywood's Wonderland, they ended in the wonder land called Australia. This posed a problem because it meant Walt's Ace had suddenly come to life and in the shape of a human, but no matter how the Mice tried to explain why they were in Australia, a Jack didn't want involvement.

Although, it wasn't a refusal to believe that was insurmountable, rather the silent one had issues and didn't realise the eerie shadow was his. In fact, the person involved only considered himself to be a normal everyday country type attempting to get out of a tight spot. So he is called Jack for the purposes of this story.

Therefore, to solve dilemmas the Mice made a bargain with an Aussie Jack or Chairman's Ace, which involved proving they could use a slick card trick to show how the former United States President had sold out Australia to anyone who wants to become say, the King or Queen of an island. Or rather than the Queen of Hearts being its Monarch, the Mice would be able to show how anyone including a terrorist sympathiser could be the new Australian Head of State. But Jack refused again because he had experienced nightmares of steel wings with invisible hands, so he remarked their game had unhappy endings.

Nevertheless, not to be outdone one of the Mice, whose name was Cliky, increased stakes by saying if a Lion agreed to help he could use a Dumbo Precedent to prove God exists and turn Jack's nightmare life into a vision of Amazing Grace with a Diamond Crown. And by this stage he believed his mind had completely gone and he was lost in cartoon woods with Mice and their slingshots anyway, so Jack reluctantly agreed. Hence, the following is how Cliky used an eerie wildcard from Elmer to find the Southern Cross and turn an Aussie Jack into a King with Wonderland's Crown ...

Gilded in Grey and Glazed by Roses

Dear God...

A FEW YEARS AGO JACK JERSUSA WAS ATTACKED by a couple of fairytales on a number of fronts, with the casualties being two taverns and no hope of securing peace in the valley. Quite simply, after discovering a limited Elephant bank had employed accountants in disguise in its credit department, Jack agreed to a settlement that was supposed to have no hangovers.

However, similar to Dumbo who believed others; he did the same and has now inherited a nightmare for a life. Problems began soon after Jack signed a Deed of Settlement with the limited bank, dear Almighty, because then it organised things so that he was blamed for all of the losses connecting the entire affair.

Therefore, it appears as if the bank's executives, officers, representatives and servants (E-ORS) weren't satisfied with destroying lives, since stealing land was also part of their Jumbo plan. Nevertheless, although their actions seemed to have had a limited amount of success, this isn't our dilemma because it is an Elephant and E-ORS problem. And because innocent Mice were also tired of being treated like fools, we decided to do something about the situation.

Thus, two relevant points which should have been considered were firstly, dear God, did the Elephant inform its fairytale agents that Jack was innocent? And, dear Worship, secondly, if Elephant Officer Lorry told Marty and Bobby that the ugly bank's lawyers had negotiated a settlement why would its agents blame an innocent person for their catastrophe? Particularly, if evidence established that the Elephant's E-ORS were dumb in their decision making. Unfortunately, the problem for the ethically challenged Elephant is the Mice only care about the first point.

And we aren't prepared to believe the E-ORS version of events since we have had enough of limited reasons, excuses, and ethics. So we are going to teach an Elephant about four other things called brains, politics, media, and then followed by the real Worship. The limited bank is a stinking mess and its E-ORS are part of it. It seems the carrots they have been munching on are magic ones that create an illusion, which portrays the Elephant as a god, but it isn't. And since this incident has happened more than once, the words mercy or forgiveness will not be applied, however God will be.

An accepted form of promotion is a business card, and on the back of an Elephant's card are the words: *professionalism and ethics in all our actions.* So if the limited bank says its tale is ethical, it must adhere to the claims because it is a requirement of law for companies to practice their preaching. One can find this information under various parts of legislation, plus one can also find many E-ORS in the case law volumes. And every time the law shows that the Jackass tale is pinned, but not like Eeyore's as in Winnie the Pooh, for the words aren't honey like your story, dear God, rather it was a muddy grey fib instead.

Sadly, after considering the behaviour of representatives so far, an Elephant's fairytale only demonstrates how agents and staffs fly under the radar. And it shows the bank has no idea its management technique causes Disneyland to deal with the issues, dear Almighty, since the bank employs many E-ORS with fairytales; therefore Eeyore the Donkey must be real!

The bank also cannot deny it allows business cards that promote false information to be freely handed out to the community, because there are E-ORS employed under disguise in its credit department to substantiate the claims. Plus, a Deed of Settlement can provide evidence showing deception as part of company policy. Thereby, proving an Elephant promotes reckless business practices by including fairytales on its business cards throughout Australia. A fact is, in August 2001, a letter providing many examples of the E-ORS' despicable management techniques and unethical stories was faxed to an Elephant CEO. But due to those fairytales now it appears the result has only meant daisies for innocent Mice.

For example, in December 2002, a Deed of Settlement revealing unethical tales by the bank's E-ORS was executed and stamped in a West Australian Court, so Marty has the evidence proving that an Elephant was at best clumsy with the business lives of innocent Mice. So why has he blamed an innocent party for insolvent trading?

Or on the other hand, perhaps the E-ORS need protection because it seems they are exposed due to a certain Elephant bank that hides under a cloud of deception by exploiting loopholes in the law? A puzzle is, if the E-ORS had read the letters disclosed by the settlement deed they would have noticed who actually caused the Dumbo atrocity, but they either cannot read or they disbelieve everyone except themselves.

So maybe it would be appropriate to teach Marty and Bobby about the word persecution, then the fall out will become catastrophic for many bank officers, via using their limited imagination with your unlimited one, dear God. For instance; if a bank supposedly believes in Australia, the Constitution, and the law it must believe in Almighty God because one cannot act within the confines of such, and then pretend that God doesn't exist otherwise, how can that be ethical?

Consequently, because Elephant lawyers Mallets Stepson with Jaques supposedly believe in God, the bank must adhere to all forms of the law and not just selective interpretations of case history. Therefore; whilst the peanut gallery and an Elephant CEO seemingly can't work it out, this doesn't mean that you cannot, dear God.

Quite simply, aside from the wayward agents, it also appears that Mallets Stepson and Jaques haven't thought about a certain deed and the letters disclosed within. Thus, the best part will be when they realise that they cannot prevent exposure of the Elephant in a certain story, so the ugly bank will have to pretend the same ignorance that executives feed Sheep. It is called grass, which seems to create illusions filled with smoky clouds of ungodlike visions.

Hence, the bank will be similar to the Sheep in its glasshouse that face public abuse because the E-ORS haven't the intestinal fortitude or strength of character to face up to reality. However, when caught; they hide behind the skirts of large law firms who haven't enough ink to sign their own names on legal stationery. It makes a Mouse click, for the executives involved in this saga appear to be an inkless mob of excuses for human beings. So welcome to the war zone, but they have picked on the wrong Mouse because he isn't stupid.

Bank lawyers insinuated the Elephant was a god by saying there would be no hangovers after executing the Deed of Settlement, which obviously meant the bank was predicting Jack's rosy future. However, the facts prove the Elephant bank isn't a god because it cannot control its own E-ORS let alone the future. But if it is proven the Elephant is a god then it unlawfully allows E-ORS to fly Jumbo kites with client assets.

Nevertheless, either way the Elephant is guilty and not a god because how can anyone be from your stable unless they are you, Lord? Further, the claim from Jack is under the structure of a deed how can it be possible to include all of the conversations over a fourteen-month settlement period? So fair play has to be included without mentioning the actual words otherwise, the document would be unworkable. This also means the bank behaving itself through agency; therefore the bank's law firm should have told Bobby and Marty to stop flying Jumbo fairytales and fix their own mess.

Please consider, dear Lord, how can the bank's agents accuse the bank's client of causing the downfall of two taverns, when the bank's senior executive of its credit department has already acknowledged the Elephant's agents were in a conflict of interest and untruthful? And why would Marty and Bobby consider blaming anyone else when their name is disclosed in clause five of the deed, and the bank has already admitted that Fairysons Chartered Accountants caused the Jumbo catastrophe?

Also, a helmet bobbles because Jack agreed to a settlement deed due to Marty and Bobby acting outside of muddy policy. But after execution, despite causing problems, the same E-ORS accuse Jack of insolvent trading, so how can their accusations be logical? Therefore, see where a bank's share price ends when we finish exposing an Elephant tale; see what the Government does when media headlines appear; see the smile on the opposition's faces in parliament; see the Elephant lawyers reach for their invisible ink; then see clowns perform in a circus as they blame each other.

Or maybe Australia will see an Elephant running as fast as it can, but unfortunately the bank will realise that like its branches it is rooted to a problem so to speak. Hence, one chainsaw started by a Mouse, then one tusk will become a glasshouse mountain. Next, observe Fairysons and Geewatahouse Chartered Accountants blame the bank to save their so-called ethical careers, for we know accountants are similar to lawyers, especially the fairies this Mouse has been introduced to.

And see bank's staff go to water and tell it like it really is, and then see a mountain that the Elephant cannot climb. Or tell Mallets Stepson with Jaques there are problems; although perhaps they may get a copy of this presentation, including teaching lessons within. Agent Marty, Officer Bobby, Geewatahouse Fairysons, and an ordinary mob of E-ORS; call themselves chartered accountants, but what do they chart apart from their own disasters? They had alleged insolvency, but in the same correspondence identify that the problems began in 1999.

Meanwhile, the so-called perpetrator was actually living in another town and never heard of the insolvent company or its taverns, because he was fixing another mess created by the business mate of Marty; namely, Mr Mountford from Mountford Chartered Accountants. And eventually, when Jack is referred to Officer Bobby in the Elephant's limited credit department because of Mountford's mess, he discovers that same Bobby is simultaneously employed by Fairysons Chartered Accountants. And it was Officer Bobby who gave Jack's file to agent Marty (his boss) to claim insolvency. Meanwhile, GeewatahouseCoopers as trustees for Mr Mountford in bankruptcy had seemingly found it difficult to investigate any circumstances in that other town.

However, the only reason Jack was involved can be attributed to the bank, because Mountford Chartered Accountants was also its client. Then finally, it is discovered that the trustees for Mountford are deployed in the limited Elephant's credit department. In other words, rose coloured glasses had been delivered to those sharing a desk in the limited Elephant's credit department, which are worn by Damwhatdeeds Bobby and Geewatahouse Marty as fairytales in disguise.

Then after their stories are told, Jack receives confirmation from Officer Lorry saying that Bobby was now a director at Fairysons and had resumed his duties at the Accounting Practice. So a Mouse wonders why there was an officer's exodus or what causes a telescope's rapid promotion. Quite simply, there is no room for cheating in sport or business because Australia means fair go; yet the bank steals a small country's name and logo, but refuses to practice its codes or rules.

Instead, hidden by invisible ink on the back of the National ugly Elephant bank's business cards isn't Almighty God's blessing or Australian morals, but an unethical limited fairytale that says ...

At the National we value (Unlimited fibs)

Service to our customers (Stealing properties)

Quality in everything we do (Fairytale accounting)

Competitiveness and a will to win (Cheating is the way)

Growing profit for our shareholders (Hidden fees and costs)

Continuous productivity improvement (Earwy fairytale training)

Growth and development of our people (Ways of tricking clients)

Professionalism and ethics in all our actions (Rose coloured stories)

P. S. ... The Jumbo Incident

(For a Few Coins More)

ONCE THERE WAS A MOUSE MINDING HIS own jungle business when two E-ORS blocked his chosen path. The Pilates (Marty and Bobby), who were flying Dumbos called Romeo and the Twin, looked down and said, "Get out of our way, pipsqueak, or we will squash you from above."

Sizing his enemy, the Mouse thought about their predicament and wondered who they were talking too. However, after looking around and finding no one else, he figured it must be him, so he asked, "Dear smarties, what has steely points with invisible hands that cast an eerie shadow?"

"That would be Dumbo," said Bobby.

"And how do you know this?" enquired the Mouse.

"Because Dumbo is a rosy Elephant with ivory tusks and earwy wings, who flies in the amazing fairytale circus from Disneyland," Marty sarcastically replied.

"But Elmo from Sesame Street said that there were a couple of Dumbos with steely points, who flew from the Holy Land then crashed somehow," mocked the Mouse.

"They were Jumbos with answers, not Dumbos with kinky tales or we would smell like daisies now," boasted Bobby.

"You don't!" roared the Mouse, "but because you flew into my story you soon will!"

Suddenly, invisible hands with steely points came crashing down.

Not long after, the Jackasses arrived at the Gates of Paradise however, before knocking on the door they saw another Mouse leaning against its walls, but on the outside. The other Mouse looked and then muttered, "Lost memories, have we?"

"What do you mean lost tales? We have been sent here by Allah," moaned Marty.

"Oh ... and how do you know this?" the Gatekeeper enquired.

"Because we have been martyred by a lyin' Mouse and his eerie Dumbo storwy about steely points with invisible hands," Bobby answered gingerly, amid obvious difficulty in making sense or forming cohesive sentences.

"What Lion Mouse?" quizzed the Gatekeeper

"The one with ivory blades and a Whale of a tale," they cried in unison.

"Well then ..." smiled the Gatekeeper, "Moby must be expecting you, so take these cards with your tails and He will stamp them with the stars."

But as they went in, to their horror they soon realised their tales were going to be pinned by the Mice in Elmer's story, you know; the one about a cwazy Wabbit with a tarred and feathered earwy Duck's shadow ...

Romeo and a Twin's Flight Plan

EAR GOD ... ANOTHER MOUSE BELIEVES ELEPHANTS are destroying our country's name by allowing their tales to crash everywhere. Obviously, it became too much to put up with because it's happened here and hear again, but the last hear wasn't reading so too bad for the E-OR Pilates. Or think France and Germany with wars one and two, the third time there won't be oil for anyone as the lights are out and nobody is home; here and hear again ...

We apologise Cliky had to grate the Elephants' brains out, although it wasn't hard to do because he was dealing with the fairytale agents. Please forgive Cliky, a Mouse in disguise of a preacher with holsters on his furry hips because he forgot who he was. The fact is we have been writing a fairytale on the way to the throne whilst Elmer and Winnie (not the real ones) were punching a Rabbit and Duck's lights out, but we knew the ending there so instead we have been playing cards; here and hear again ...

Meaning; we have been putting a few words and puzzles together, but it isn't a laughing game for the moral is a David and Goliath story. That is throw the rock, grate a big guy, then ask questions. Alas, Cliky had forgotten this meant black eye and like David missed. But while David is a hero, a Mouse hopes the sitting Ducks in parliament know what a giant means because Walt isn't prejudiced either; here and hear again ...

Here, two grated Elephants, including the daisies as the Mice couldn't sweep out the mess since there weren't any brooms left. Cliky lost his cool when they wouldn't listen for the tenth time, so he informed a bank by a broom handle. Then he became a Bull in a china shop and the broken glass caused their kites to fall out of the sky. And guess what? Luci was right; plastic doesn't fly unless it's full of hot air, but block your nose if the air smells because Elmer attacked, and then a Duck and Rabbit found themselves, here and hear again ...

We also heard Luci saw how quickly the statues went with everything else. Thus, those Dumbos copped a lode from the slingshot and tons of rubble went their way, so a large plate of good cheese is coming back for the Mouse's reward. Obviously, the Elephant's gang weren't reading the newspaper, since it was the Mouse who knocked out two countries in a race to grab the diamonds because they failed to remember who was driving a Lorry in the way. The method used was via a deed, but they broke it and Jack didn't; here and hear again ...

Furthermore, the Dumbo bank preaches truth on its business cards, but the fairytales operating it are the same in ethical stature as the false representation they carry. And any Mouse can rip a bank statue in half, roll it up and set fire to it because there isn't much of a smell and only a short burn with nothing left after. Go to any branch and get one, they give them out for free because they don't know what their business cards mean either; here and hear again ...

Banks think they can put Australia's name after theirs such as the Commonwealth and National. But apart from it is a nation that comes after Australia what has national got to do with anything? Surely, it's we die for our country and not our country dies for us? So similar to the ANZ bank and realise that in the long term we still flog New Zealand at cricket, banks should not put our name behind theirs until they know Australia comes first. Ask any cricketer what's better, National Australia Captain or Australia's National Captain; here and hear again ...

In closing, a Mouse says the E-ORS forgot to do one up and caused an Elephant trip similar to a grass one. Meaning they thought they were flying, but the result was two Pilates with broken tales. So due to fairytales on business cards here is another melted story, however, please forgive Cliky. But there should be no leniency for the limited bank called Romeo, because there aren't any credits in that corporation only wasted trips and E-ORS with Dumbo fairytales, **yours faithfully dear Almighty ...**

Memo ... The Dumbo Declaration

DEAR GOD ... Another Mouse referred to the above and declared a fairytale war.

- **Explanation:** No broom handles left so Cliky said use Elephant Tusks
- **Orders:** Job access via the Angel's Business Card and Stone Thrower
- **Decree:** When dealing in all things Elephant ... Pray for the lawyers
- **Mouse Duty:** Submit with Jackasses (edited) because it seems these E-ORS are similar to those in Iraq. In other words, their tales have also been pinned to the card printed in spades and stamped with the Dumbo stars; so Walt wasn't happy either ...
- **Story:** 'E-OR Pilates' flying Elephant kites
- **Plot:** Broken Deed of Settlement
- **Excuse:** Memory Failure
- **Surrender Plans:** One
- **Pity for the E-ORS:** Perhaps
- **Pity for Elephants:** None
- **Humour:** Read on
- **Injuries:** Tin Man (not the real one!) smashed by Moby's Rock Stars
- **Swear Words:** Their Oath and Affirmation; then just the 'O'
- **Classification Ratings:** Two
- **PG Reason:** Kinky Tales Pinned by Jumbo Nails via Moby's Slingshot
- **M Reason:** A Long Rubber Band
- **True or False:** Both
- **Evidence:** Included

- **Mouse Disguise:** Allah knows
- **Tactics:** Fairytales pinned to Broken Stories
- **Result:** Exposed their Roman Memories
- **Subject:** Romeo's Twin flying in Sesame Street's Concrete Jungle
- **Lesson:** The Lights were on in 'Australia, but not Georgia'
- **Mouse Cost:** Double the other Number
- **Elephant Cost:** Romeo and the Twin
- **Fictional Ending:** Letting Tin Man (not the real one!) work it out
- **Factual Ending:** Politicians with Bushy Kangaroo Tales
- **Weapons of Mass Destruction:** Two Business Cards

Reasons for using the Heavenly Cannons are ...

The Man of Steel's X-Ray Vision

*I*N NOVEMBER 2003, INSTEAD OF BEING ABLE to redeem losses caused by Fairysons, Jack had to file a fairytale claim in the Federal Court for it seemed that Prime Minister Howard had infracted upon the rules (Ten Commandments) that govern God's blessing in the Constitution Act. And also, those duties imposed by the coronation oath upon the Queen as Head of the Church of England and Australia.

Prime Minister Howard or as the US President called him, the 'man of steel', made an address to the nation on 20 March 2003. This speech concerned reasons Australian forces were supporting a United States led coalition of the willing to invade Iraq. In his speech Mr Howard claimed that Iraq had weapons of mass destruction and posed an imminent threat to Australia and the rest of the world.

Unfortunately there were no weapons of mass destruction, so it meant Mr Howard's decision was also religiously unconstitutional because Australian souls were at risk, since their armed forces had invaded a country for no Godlike reasons. So Jack had to deliberately lose a court case, and then spend years of his life researching how to fix infractions that required the Commonwealth Executive to repair rather than him.

And evidence the God in the Constitution Act can't save a soldier's soul is clear, as Mr Howard ignored the royal prerogative in 2003, and in doing so implied that God's blessing was no longer a constitutional requirement. But Jack was not amused, as it meant a sacrifice of some sort would have to be made to protect Australians.

And to ensure evidence was reliably recorded he also had to include a number of particulars that would substantiate his intention of deliberately filing an unwinnable court claim (QUD 171/2003). Filing of the claim was before it had been revealed Iraq had no weapons of mass destruction.

The reason he chose a metaphorical sacrifice (forgiveness rule), was if Mr Howard was wrong about Iraq, Australian souls could be at risk since the royal prerogative was ignored. And since previous facts about Iraq's weapons suggested Mr Howard was wrong; a risk to Australian souls arose in 2003, because the Queen's Crown could be proven as unconstitutional by a citizen sympathetic to the cause of Islamic terrorists. Thereby, to ensure protection for Australian souls it was paramount that Jack's actions were reliably recorded.

As a result, on 10 November 2003, Jack filed a claim against the National bank and Fairysons. Relevant orders sought were;

- Removal of the word Australia from the bank's trading name.
- Permission to publish a manuscript titled *The Angel's Business Card*.
- Compensation for losses caused by Fairysons.

It was obvious the Federal Court did not have jurisdiction in any of the orders sought. Therefore, on 05 February 2004, the claim was dismissed. However, the reality is Jack's purpose was to record evidence, whilst also instigating a situation where, in theory at least, the court had to 'wash its hands of the affair'. Thus, Jack manipulated proceedings due to the strange circumstances originally causing the need for a deed with the bank, the terminology used during the negotiating period and also, a set of strange events that happened within a short time after the deed's execution. These events provided spiritual evidence to suspect that two Prime Minsters' decisions to commit forces to invade Iraq had caused the Crown to be unconstitutional.

Suddenly, a Heavenly Pin-Up Card was added to their memos to God ...

From the Twins Ivory

(Edged in Grey and Decorated with Rosy Stars)

EAR GOD ... ONE WOULD THINK ALICE KNOWS WHAT your blessing means. As you know, Tin Man ignored the Queen's royal prerogative which means by law you weren't consulted at all, but yet Elmer and Winnie (not the real ones) said that you told them to do it after their fibs were exposed. How is that legally possible?

Clearly, it seems Tin Man was consulted first and his x-ray vision was used to verify Iraq's weapons, instead of your vision, dear God. Perhaps this explains why they call Tin Man the 'man of steel', particularly if thinking about who takes the blame for not reading a Constitution's large print; seems like a Dumbo betrayal of you, Lord.

Anyhow, in his letters Jack had started referring to Elephants because he appeared to be sick of E-ORS. And in August 2001, when he had to go West, Jack allowed friends stay in his apartment. Then upon returning after attempting to fix an ordinary effort from the Dumbos, as a thankyou gift his friends had left a drawing of a woman, so Jack hung it above the computer. And as time went by the lady in a frame was able to witness many Mouse type letters.

However, after a while he switched tactics and started writing to the E-ORS and you, dear God, but sometimes the letters were never sent because Jack felt that you had already read them. Then in April 2002, he walked into a bar and was served by a woman who seemed similar to the drawing in his apartment. And ultimately, meeting her provided an opportunity to invest in a business called Mary Street Nightclub, but unfortunately because of allegations from the Elephant's agents that investment opportunity also disappeared, dear Lord.

By this stage Jack's company Burymore was liquidated and he was facing financial ruin, though undeterred he attempted to invest in a restaurant in Toowong, but alas due to other E-ORS an argument also occurred over the truth. This problem happened in March 2003, but the events were triggered in February.

Jack was celebrating a return to normality and commiseration for Miss Mary's Nightclub when a pretty woman walked into his life. And as stated before, her line was, "never stand in the way of a girl trying to get to the bar." Nevertheless, it seemed the joke also amused Jack even though it wasn't surprising or original worshipping.

Then after the pretty lady gave him a business card and said that it was false, the next week Jack and the fake card spent a fair amount of time on the phone. But at that stage he did not know about the impending disaster from Toowong or any decisions from the pretty lady and her lemon card. Furthermore, even though the lady was on holidays, since Jack was working on business plans to save a restaurant he wasn't able to meet, so apparently the phone had to do.

Anyway, eventually the lady mentioned she was going out for dinner and would be at the Regatta the following Friday. Therefore, because he wanted to watch Australia in the World Cricket Final on the hotel's big screen television, Jack arranged to meet her. Nonetheless, during the time leading up to their meeting Jack talked about a poem called Among the Multitude, which is a simple structure of eight or nine lines, but its contents have many meanings, dear Lord.

Basically, a poem is about meeting someone and that person has prior knowledge as to why they have met you. In other words fate and déjà vu, or the reference isn't just about fate because it includes déjà vu. This means both have to be the component for one of the parties to have any idea of an impending significant moment in the life of the other. The singer Cheryl Crow wrote about the poem, and as you know the song became a live tour favourite, dear God.

Hence, by the time Friday arrived Jack began to have feelings of being somewhere before and felt an impending disaster. Mainly because when he was watching the cricket with a couple of friends, he received a text message from the pretty woman asking for the score. So he replied with another message saying that it was raining sixes at the Regatta, but inadvertently he also forgot to mention what her final score was, dear Lord.

Then later that evening the prophetic words seem to reveal themselves when a painted business card told Jack that hope valley wasn't going to be a part of the equation. Although, at the same time the woman also said she had never connected with someone so quickly and still wanted him to call her. However, a card with a puzzle as its logo was the only thought on Jack's mind, and as for the painted lady it wasn't what she said because it was the way she said it.

Alas, the answer from him wasn't expected for although she wanted friendship, the wounded soul only received thorns. And he left after hearing a cliché line from the consultant, because whilst it appeared Jack may have been disappointed with the situation, his heart knew that her answer didn't mean having no future.

Perhaps a reason may have been because of what was inside the business card, dear Lord. Also, notwithstanding one's ordinary deception to the pretty woman, an individual had no doubt that meeting her was a profound moment in his life. Although, at the time he couldn't explain why and instead believed that whatever path he chose in the future would be the right one. Maybe it was a picture hanging on the wall and Mary's Nightclub that provided a clue?

Besides, by the time March arrived Toowong had become a disaster, so Jack sent roses with thorny pages to a painted lady; all of which had been compliments from the results of meeting the pretty woman. And as the months went by many versions of the complaint were sent to her employer and various other authorities, but no reply was received from the card.

So Jack thought he had better write properly and include Mice in his story, namely Cliky and his band. Perhaps it wasn't what he was writing, but it was the way he wrote it. And this may have been caused by a business card or picture's indifference to the matter. Although, one didn't care because he had faith in what he was doing, but on many occasions things became difficult as prejudgments flowed.

Then soon Jack stopped thinking about the mortgage because she didn't want to know him anyway, so the Mice burned the card and then destroyed its evidence, but only stopped as results announced an impending event, dear Lord. Eventually, after gaining the upper hand a notice was delivered by a ringing doorbell at Heaven's gate. So Cliky accepted the notice because one had a feeling that he was about to go from a Jack to a King.

However, during a moment with the pretty woman a thought occurred to the no-funny-business Mouse. Jack talked about what sort of music he enjoyed so the woman replied she liked Tears for Fears and everybody wants to rule the world. Then Jack replied that he liked U2, so she answered the singer of the band was sexy. His name is Bono, but he isn't you, Lord.

Obviously, this was to Jack's liking so he talked about music and the song dealing with a couple of others known as Judas and Jesus. It's about the Act of Jesus and the events leading into the Crucifixion. The song is called until the end of the world or something. Eventually, time drifted by before Jack realised hadn't been interrupted so he asked the pretty lady if he was boring her. But she responded with the comment it's not what you say, it's the way you say it. Also, she said that she thought 2wong was cute, dear God.

Afterwards, in between the time of the picture with Miss Mary's Nightclub and leaving a lady at the Regatta; Pashen and Cliky arrived. Although Jack continued to pursue a pretty woman with fake romantic interest but thankfully, at no stage did she attempt a joke about getting to his bar again. Cliky believes it may have been the flowers and evidence that he sent displaying the drama she had left behind, because this seemed to ensure the business card wasn't going to come back. And one kept on working so it was impossible for Cliky to be interested in any offer apart from her worshipping or resignation from all claims in the affair, dear Lord.

So considering Jack has been liquidated, but the events have proven it was a waste at the time. Coupled with the fact that at worst evidence as contained within the Cliky complaint points to a conspiracy theory born from ignorance on a grand scale? Plus, thinking of the lady and her views about the situation because it will be proven that she disappeared also; a tail has been wondering is the woman entitled to any of the prayer pleadings, dear Lord?

This brings the Mouse to some other points because the thinking involving two issues has drawn strength from a Colosseum of events from Jack and Cliky's view. And despite that an Elephant bank is in for a headache by the Cliky complaint, a 'Heavenly Pin-Up Mouse' has also been thinking about a few other things as well, Lord. For example, if Cliky Mouse is a registered trading entity formed through inspiration from meeting a painted woman at Miss Mary's Nightclub, which led to the lemon with a puzzle; then legally speaking isn't a Mouse entitled to be alive and breathing?

Meaning trading on a daily basis including writing books and other ventures, otherwise it will have to be more than the stated compensation. Or equating to adding the recurring three with no decimal point; but a whale of a tale since it's about Allah, Moses, Jesus, and Judas, followed by Jacobs and Jones worshipping the dear Honours.

Also, apart from frosty endeavours Jack hasn't contacted the lady thereby; proving this story is factual and not like some of the other fairytales flying about the place. And while Cliky was borne from her business card, unfortunately the pain afterwards resulted in terrible labours, so at best their meeting was lemon scented. Further, from Cliky's view if he kept the Mice in luxury from compensation of say forty-five million cheeses, does this also mean that he has to pay alimony amounts?

Besides, at the end of the day although it was a meeting borne from an inspiration, it meant Jack was left minding a babe and not her, dear Lord. Nevertheless, a pretty woman approached a man and introduced herself saying she is a single girl with a mortgage; then said she had never connected with someone so quickly, but changed her mind. Therefore, what do you think she was saying about the guy she saw at the Cinema Café because she appeared to be whispering about him to her unlucky friend?

Perhaps she may have been saying that since she met Jack he has kept her baby and the labour pains. And she may have said he has educated a Mouse so he knows a bit about law; taught him how accountants add up; and cheese grated the Elephant via the kinky tale method from a fairytale den? Plus, with a tiny bit of Amazing Grace, Cliky has earned three hundred million cheeses whilst crusading against the E-ORS in Australia. Considering the previous, wouldn't people think the lady with the false card was saying that a Mouse is the one that got away?

Apparently, she told Jack she lived in Bulimba, but sips her coffee at Morningside. So as a peace offering should Cliky give her the Mouse size alimony of say, nothing? This would keep her and the mortgage on mourning's side, whilst still pretending to have a life at the coffee shop across the road from the Cinema Café. But would it be the right thing to do, because the Mice don't want a pretty woman who thinks she rules the world on our doorstep! So if you think it would be the best punishment for the card, Lord, we agree as Cliky wants to stay with Jack, which includes taking the loot with him! **Yours truly dear God and to be continued ...**

P. S. ... Interview with a Mouse

LORIST: "SO WHY DID YOU ADD YOUR CARDS to the Dumbo Precedent?"
Pashen: "It's our credentials for the other royal positions just in case they cannot find anybody."

Florist: "Oh ... I see ... is this because someone doesn't want the job?"

Pashen: "Yep, but England may need a safety net so the other Mouse and I have enclosed our credentials, which are hidden in this tale like the Parliamentary gobbledygook, hear and hear."

A florist raised her eyebrows, shook her head in mock disbelief and smiled as she added the business cards to the bouquets. And later that evening in whispered tones Mice spoke about a Ferryman and lost crew setting sail from Gallipoli. But as the light from their lamp shone on top of dark waters, you could see an eerie reflection of the Southern Cross leading the way; whilst carrying the keys to freedom for a sunburnt country's Anzac smiles and diamond hearts.

Although, among the Mice it was agreed the real victim is democracy since Liberty is a statue everyone throws stones at. And most times those in her heart have to rely on themselves because who else is there? Usually, this means if America helps the world they get abused and if they don't help, it's the same. So they turn their cheeks until it's unbearable, which occasionally involves an Emperor somewhere saying he should be running things, or the West is corrupt. But the Emperor doesn't behave like the true hero in winning office; rather, power is obtained by the barrel of a gun.

Therefore, unless we want to believe that terrorism is right, the reason why Two Towers fell down was God didn't help for He wants a change, but He has also provided a warning about what path the world is taking. Or conversely, God isn't complicated, but the answers aren't simple.

And none more so in reasons of war, especially when one side of religion claims they're doing it for Allah; whilst the other uses false excuses involving weapons. And because neither side was telling the truth, the real Ace embarrasses everyone, whilst providing permission for Cliky to smash two Elephants without death.

Therefore, who hid their cheese? A fact is God knew there weren't weapons of mass destruction and Saddam had skeletons underground before terrorist activity. So to open skeleton closets God gave a Mouse His keys forged by Diamonds from Gallipoli, but in the process He has also reminded that lest we forget a Texas Ranger and his Deputies made errors.

"Oh, no they didn't," bleated Sheep from the Union Jack.

"Yes they did," growled a Wolf in his wig.

"How can that be?" chorused the Animal Farm chewing grass from the other side.

"Because God said," whispered a Shadow blocking the Son.

"What God?" asked the Phoenix covered in ashes.

"The One that was stuck on a Cross," said Unicorns in the playground.

"Why isn't He there?" sang Halos from the blue sky.

"Because Judas has escaped again," said Jackasses flying kites.

"Who let him through the noose?" enquired the Flower in her tower.

"We think it was Allah," replied the Jumbo with neon lights.

"No it was the Python in a Mercedes," said the Prophet to the Hobbit.

"Oh they must be false," bragged an Actor with fire and glass.

"Definitely right," replied a Cartoon character from Hollywood.

"Can you wash the children's hands?" asked Alice whilst she was preparing dinner.

"Not now, we are watching TV," scowled President Brady.

"Oh, what's on; Shrek and the Donkey or Mickey with Pluto?" enquired the Tea Party from Wonderland.

"Neither," said the stars with the CEO, but added, "We see it but don't believe it, a Mouse has won a diamond from the Queen by playing the Jack of Hearts and King of Spades with Romeo and the Twin's fairytale from Disneyland, what's next, dear God?"

P.S.S. ...

A Prayer 4 U2 Stuff Elephants and E-ORS Without Leaving an Island ...

For Their Sad Days

Australia is an acrobat and everyone wants to rule the world however, a Jack doesn't want to be an Angel of Harlem. And although it's a beautiful day desire isn't better than the real thing because Ireland wants to find Jesus. But they still haven't found what they are looking for so perhaps in a little while God will move in mysterious ways. Jersusa wasn't New Year's Day or a zoo station with a miner's passion, but like the fly he went to stay in a land far away so close. And if wild honey's the sweetest thing until the end of the world then what happens on a day when the Elephants come to town? England had the signs for the streets with no name, although she can't find who rode the wild horses with or without a new star. And a Jack wasn't the fourth of July or a sort of home coming, but it wasn't bad because Australia under an Indian summer sky solved a puzzle. So the Queen found rain from MLK because Jersusa's star on the promenade had the unforgettable fire. Therefore, a Mouse sent an email so Liberty could throw her arms around the missing Mice, for a Jack knows her thoughts are love is blindness and not everybody wants to rule the world. But if Two Towers weren't so cruel or in the name of a freedom ring then like ultra violet there were bullets in the blue sky because Elvis is a rock that can't sing. And when the Jumbos overlooked one tree hill, Liberty's reply didn't fail to see him running to stand still. Born from a red hill mining town Jack didn't trip on their wires because his choice was a tree without elevation. Then to mine a heart so freedom could walk on wild honey the Queen needed a card to play her game. But the Joshua tree alone in the Regatta was a Spade. And a black Jack wasn't in a lonesome way or to be her wild honey in a peanut bar. So a game with false statues began and the Jack proved he was the best against the Elephant with a star. Yes, the trumps were in Liberty's cards, Mr Jaques, because the King's sling doesn't march to the tune of a club. So Al Qaeda had a dance not once but twice with a Jumbo lance, that was stolen from freedom blades as they ran into Grace and His Invisible Hands. Then an Elephant became no challenge like rattle and hum when its stars faced the Spade with an Ace's gun. But we don't know if God is here anymore because the truth wasn't the reason for their law. Perhaps they saw gold beneath the land, but at the same time there wasn't an excuse for the pilot gang. And Mice are tired of kinky tales flown with iron intellects, but not the gold album that sells without a voice because he can hear music and understand the word God. Though, would it be unwise if a Jack said there is room in his heart for Amazing Grace instead? Yes we know Jacobs is a clown and with the agents two burnt down. But weren't you ashamed when you heard a scream as Two Towers crashed and it was no dream. Or was that Liberty with a tear in her eye as the world saw her desperate Mice try to fly. So please say we fight in the name of their sad days. And keep singing Bono with a gang of three, since the world hasn't understood, dear God please. She loves our music, but at the end of the day a world has a troublesome kink; which means lose our cards printed in black and stamped with red ink. Although, perhaps it's best to see an Owl for an Elephant to understand that Liberty's one and only statue is Amazing Grace with Invisible Hands, Amen. **Please save our Mice, dear God, and thanks to the Irish crew ...**

Yours Faithfully

Cliky, Pashen, and the Other Mouse

The Funeral for His Friend

One day as God and Liberty were hovering above the clouds, counting hearts from holy ground; the horny one posed a question, "Lord, why is it you never tell the tale about Grace and the King with no wedding ring?" God smiled and replied, "perhaps you would like a game of cards and if you win then you can join me again?' Lucifer responded; "Agreed, however during our game maybe the story from a Jack to a King should be told."

God replied, "Yes, why not play Bridge whilst a storyteller recites the fable of a Mouse and foe, but let's use cards from the real world and watch them slide, then we shall see who told fibs and who told lies. Also, if he solves the riddle from a Jack to a King with no wedding ring the world will see our light again. And if the Mouse under the tree can rise in thee, Australia will save a Queen through Liberty. Nevertheless, if they play the wrong way His Thorns will bloom from a slave and soon they will see who dances in the dark with the Black Knave."

But then Almighty God added, "Also understand that he will quote a Bible with their game plan, followed by an answer to a riddle that says: If the player checks within they will notice the book has no end, but inside the Holy Scrolls are words that mean they mustn't tamper with its soul. However, to win you must seek from an enemy's sleep."

Lucifer thought for a minute and hissed, "Perhaps we should play for the old stakes instead." God responded, "No Luci, you made the play, so a game of life is in your hands today." Therefore, clouds were arranged for Angels to converge on whilst the one in the robe recited the tale about the joker and thief.

Meanwhile, Dumbo Pilates shuffled, "Jersusa's unit is eleven, Jersusa's address is at unit eleven, Jersusa's address should be unit nine, but it's unit eleven. The address where Jersusa lives is unit eleven; Jersusa's address isn't unit nine because Jersusa's address is unit eleven. If Jersusa's address wasn't at unit eleven, perhaps it would be unit nine. Maybe he lives in eleven, but his address is nine eleven."

Again the Dumbos echoed, "Burymore's unit is eleven, Burymore's address is eleven, Burymore's address should be unit nine, but it's unit eleven. The address where Burymore should be is unit eleven. Burymore's address isn't unit nine because Burymore's address is unit eleven. If Burymore's address wasn't at unit eleven, perhaps it would be unit nine eleven."

Then their game began and Luci led with wildcards from a blue sky. Suddenly, the world cried as they watched their desperate Mice try to fly. But before the Heavens began to sing an Angel was sent to find Jack and the King. However, as per usual Saint Peter was crowing instead of confessing, so rather than being in another space, the Mouse ended in a regatta race. Although, for the moment Luci smiled at the tales glowing in the night, for the stories began twisting by the results of his delight. And soon laughter echoed beneath the ground, sending fear into the streets as confusion raged all round.

So the fairytale agents sang, "Jack lives in number seven, Jack's address is at seven. However, Jack's address should be unit ten, but it's unit seven. The place where Jack might live is unit ten. If Jack's address wasn't at unit seven, perhaps it would be ten. Maybe he lives in unit seven, but his address is unit ten."

Then on an island lightning crashed whilst thunder roared as a nightclub and restaurant were destroyed. Although, when the crowds converged around they found their roses beneath holy ground. So a Mouse turned towards the sky and sent a prayer to Amazing Grace with Godlike eyes, because an Aussie had a frown when they played the card from Wonderland's Crown.

"Dear God … a Mouse is only the gatekeeper so why have you summoned him? What is your desire and command for he has committed many sins, learned from them and asked for your forgiveness, so how is that not your way? Lay the Mouse in your arms when he is weak, but not in the arms of an Elephant that pretends he is you, Lord.

"If the Mouse has committed a sin against the Romans then you punish his life, but not the Elephant because a Lion is better than the Elephant. We are in your hands because He became lost in the maze for you, so how can we be perfect when you have provided the temptation? Please tell us why the Romans are accusing this Mouse, dear God?

"You were the Mouse and Lion in the Colosseum not the Elephant, so why are these Romans persecuting our Mice, dear Lord? He has been sent among us to expose the crimes, so why is this Mouse involved in their mess, and why have you summoned him to the traps of nothing? Have we not walked among the sinners and prayed for their forgiveness as well as our own? Have we not held your hand during the fires of hell, and you ours, Almighty God?

"And have we not screamed your name in pain whilst condemning the dark, and cried for your suffering at the gates of destruction; so why this Mouse here? What right has this Elephant to uncover the Keeper? Are these stones the ones, or are they just another bridge until you deliver us from evil? Who are these stones for, dear Almighty God?

"Will your faith rescue us from deliverance, and will your passion rescue us from persecution whilst washing the hands of the innocent? Will your life be mine and mine yours or will they do what you declare, as you do for us, God? And will they light the fires of hell on the ice of life, or pour the water onto our burning innocence; as you do for us, dear Almighty? Time will tell, Lord, time will tell."

Luci looked at God and down at Jack again, the Snake showed sweet delight as he said, "I think I have made an enemy for you, my friend." But God smiled and replied; "See the Mouse with a frown and see his heart shattered on the ground, the mistake was yours, dear Snake, you forgot thy enemy is the Keeper of the Gate. Please don't go because there's more come, so let's watch the Mouse do his work and have some fun. For the Deed of Settlement has been broken, can't you see, come, and let us hear Jack recall an Elephant history."

So when the Ace looked down at a Jack on the ground, He sent the roses with a Thorny Crown. But inside the flower's Roman coat was an inscription Luci had wrote: "It's raining at the Regatta, can't you see; please take care of this card for me." However, soon a wicked smile creased the Australian's face as he read the other message from Amazing Grace, "The Aces have gone, her hearts are Knaves, so the Kings have first order because the precedent's arranged."

Then as we saw her watch him from the corners of her eyes, she stood by a doorway whilst her friends played with fires. So her friends said to him she's an angel in disguise, but alas, they didn't notice; the sword was his only vice. Soon we saw Unicorns and heard their laughter. Nonetheless, the joker smiled as he whispered to a thief, "You take the left side, for I will take the right, and let's play the crossing game to see what lies beneath."

And when she touched his hand it was cold as ice, but it felt like home to the thief wearing his disguise. Nevertheless, as her game switched from fire to statues in the sand, Jack just laughed, and drew a cross with a fool's plan. So then we sang, "Please don't forsake her if you're a thief or a joker; and don't you forget him if you're a joker or a thief; for although your game of fools is for a Potter's keep, it was the joker who danced on water in her restless sleep."

Next, we saw that in her bouquet of roses went a poetry lesson, which was written with an ivory lance and fuelled by a two-way dimension. But its purpose for the joker wasn't a test, because rumour has it their future was predicted without a guess. Although, the truth was it was sent by a thief more or less, but anyway; laughter had replaced the grin by the time a joker had sent her roses and kept a thorny note within.

Besides, they claimed that it was from her tower where they heard the thief whisper, "One doesn't care who cleans the disgrace because it shouldn't have been there in the first place. And when Jersusa finds a solution but is cut at the knees so to speak, then my temper starts to leak. Above all; when a Mouse writes to Elephants and instead they send lawyers in a coat, then muddy water is the order, that's what Amazing Grace had wrote."

"A man is tired of running into cards who talk or pictures that walk. And the real Ace has had enough of E-ORS with false titles and politicians with brains of straw, because it was the Mouse who remembered without prejudice whilst the guilty hid behind Liberty's front door. So Jack, here's my message straight from Moses to you, it takes ten steps via the Judge before William and the Holy crew."

"Firstly, negotiate at a meeting because one enjoys adding a face to the shell that's going to be fired, and then shake a lawyer's hand to feel what isn't inside. But when the others play their game, find the Mouse that watches whilst a King plays another, which isn't the same. Then soon it will be their stars that have to take the blame. Nonetheless, because our temper is completely astray, unfortunately it also doesn't end here. So let a Mouse write his fairytale for everyone to laugh at the silly games preachers and Unicorns fear."

Meanwhile, the Elephant announced a new plan, too bad it was via an old sound, although it was predictable their kites had to land. Anyway; perhaps it wasn't a silly silk cord because the order came from a chair and board. But they were too late, for Jack saw an ivory with a fiddle, so he split their rhinestones down the middle.

And through the night Heaven sang and lighting flashed as fire and thunder exploded. Because when the statues marched, their band played on the wings of defeat, and as their tails turned we saw the flowers wilt from the heat. Then through New York eyes, we saw glass roses shattered on the street. Although Jack played a joker, whilst the thief smiled at the players from the sand, for he wasn't a time waster, so he kept an Ace for a Queen's plan.

Besides, they were from the false cards and blessed without a Holy thought. Therefore, smash them with a zero and then cross them with Allah's naught. Suddenly, we heard Luci scream with delight as God played a dummy and Allah ducked out of sight. Because although his time had almost come, for them it meant the unforgettable fire had not been won. And Luci hissed, "A nightmare is theirs today because they took Jumbos and paid with glass for their flying lessons in September anyway."

"So how's your conscience today, or will your demons chase it away? Because we laughed as they climbed the mountain, heard their leaders as they filled their fountain; they used their coins of right or wrong although it seems it was an unhappy love song." And then he sang; "Please don't forsake him if you're a thief or a joker; and don't you forget her if you're a joker or a thief; for although your game of fools is for a Potter's keep, it was the joker who danced on water in her restless sleep."

Next we said, "To Moses Mouse at Heaven's Gate, it's a bank's funeral with its silly mates. We did it with a sling to a rhinestone pin, then via a Cat who knows how to sing. From the media's page came the cartoon's ace and in Court sat a red rose in black lace. To the left were lawyers without a face because Jack had a Dumbo Precedent and everything was erased. That's why we trick E-ORS in disgrace and pin their tales with Amazing Grace."

"For when the Judge shuffled the leaves we found an Ace in the dealer's sleeve, but the editors didn't care because they won a war and the weapons weren't there. It's a shame they can't understand that sometimes Elephants are Romans in this land. And just because Jacobs wasn't visible too, there isn't an excuse for what Jones flew. Yes they listened and filled a fountain, with Osama's ideas of right or wrong; and now Iraq's children are the unhappy love song."

Again the Elephant announced another man, too bad it was via the limited crown, although it was predictable their rhetoric had to land. Anyway; perhaps it wasn't the silly silk's chord because the order came from a chair and board. But they were too late, for the King saw an ivory with a fiddle so He split their rhinestones down the middle. And we heard; "Please don't forsake him if you're a thief or a joker; and don't you forget her if you're a joker or a thief."

Mimicked the Handle to the Spade? Because when a Queen shuffled the leaves we found an Ace in the dealer's sleeve, but the editors didn't care because they won a war and the weapons weren't there. It's a shame they can't understand that sometimes politicians are Romans in our land. And just because martyrs were guilty too, there wasn't an excuse for the lies that England flew. Yes, Australia listened and filled its fountain, with American coins of right or wrong; and now Iraq's children are the unhappy love song.

Then we heard; "There she goes with another fan, she lost a friend but they say she understands. And newspapers claim the priest wasn't a man, so he shouldn't prey in church because it wasn't the plan. Where's Allah or where did He go, still grieving from the Crucifixion of Jesus we suppose? Why not ask the children because they weren't fooled, there wasn't any God during Sunday school? Still they listened and filled their fountain with another idea of right or wrong; too bad it's an unhappy love song."

Sang the skeleton from a closet? For when they flew statues with neon lights from a poison desert Mister, above the clouds it's rumoured the Angels heard His black heart whisper, "P.S. Jack, once there was a man who was blessed as a country, followed by a Whale that taught the Pharaoh the dangers of a Red Sea. Next the Carpenter who crossed a bridge for humanity, but in between those times there was a slinger who taught Goliath dignity."

"For their funeral friend, please keep swinging the blade at the Elephant until the end. Then one day the peanuts will understand that it's the King of Spades who stands by Liberty's right hand. Don't fear the Romans on the left side because they are only here to pay for souls and wash their hands of a Jumbo lie. But if the Queen provides a reason why, bow gracefully; and then use the blessing on which Australians rely."

"Their hearts were shattered because they didn't understand, but it wasn't our fault because we weren't in their plan. If you want advice think about an enemy's sleep or being cold as ice. The way to expose the truth is via Goliath's sling; or swim down a river, and find our clues, hidden in the poems by the hand of a Shepherd King. And whilst the card might be like no other its puzzle wears a red gown, so don't let the false star drive you down."

"A preacher says one thing but does another, whilst a statue is ripped apart as the gun destroys a heart. Nonetheless, the silly peashooters forgot one thing; that it's the duty of the Mouse to bury every Jacobs and Jones in this story who think their Elephant's king."

"And although Jesus is the Son of God, he's still only dear God's Son and in reality, a Jack. So until someone proves otherwise, then say Amazing Grace with Godlike eyes is the only statue this Mouse bows to, Mr Jaques. Therefore, the Unicorns with a statue and false crown can play in some other frosty playground because this sword has two blades. Firstly, the Romans broke an agreement in the past and secondly, they broke it in the present. Leading to a bright future for you, but not the E-ORS with their unfaithful Elephants."

Thus, the twenty fifth day fell silent at their unholy place, but God wasn't a fool because He saw their stars had acted in disgrace. So Jack played the King from the land down under, since the Mouse had brought His Crown from beneath the rosy tree thereafter. For the points of its thistles were pinned to an Ace that whispered from within its thorny vine, "This is for them because they were only boys dressed as men, who ended as ghosts to haunt Australia's mind."

So we sang, "To the lawyer Jaques with their man, remember when we freed your country from an Achtung band. This is for Pashen's Mouse in sunburnt land, with his jigsaw card and Roman gang's confession, that says why Mice cross banks with Liberty's permission, and trick agents that fly kinky tales on the island. But if terrorists take Jumbos and pay in glass for their flying lessons, then we use Amazing Grace and edge His shells with a drumbeat from Heaven."

In the end Luci stayed and smiled with glee as the statues were torn in half by Jersusa and Cliky. Then Grace laughed at the Jacobs' frown when Jack gave the Mouse a diamond with his thorny crown. Although, perhaps the politicians and scribes will say it wasn't the Judge with a ladder, because the mistake came from the capital; the one near the river, close to a ford but shaped at a right angle.

However, the Mice will say it was an Aussie Jack who bowed with style, then holstered his sword and flew into the arms that held her amazing smile. And sometimes during the night, perhaps it will be whispered that as the black rose fell from His gown, "a smile hadn't left the Mouse King with the Diamond in His Thorny Crown."

P. S. ... Good Rockin' Tonight

"CLIKY YOU HAVE NAILED IT AGAIN!" said Dumbo, Winnie, Eeyore, and Owl (the real ones).

"P. S. ... Pinned it!" added Postman Pat with his letters.

"Sorry I was late, but on the way to Grandma's my attention was captured by Cliky's fairytale," the girl in a red riding hood explained to a surprised Inspector with Gadgets.

"I had a fairytale in bed with Grandma," said a laughing Wolf.

"Oh dear, Romeo has slipped up again!" giggled a Banana in Pyjamas.

"Wins the letter of the day," smiled a presenter on Play School.

"It tricked Bert," smiled Ernie with a Big Bird from Sesame Street.

"I wonder if the circus will ever get its fairytale crown again," thought the Ringmaster.

"Peace and the cake!" thumped Moby to the beat of 'American Pie'.

"I hope he doesn't rock the boat," said Mickey to Donald with Minnie and Daisy in Disneyland.

"Will Cliky's Whale of tale end in Hollywood?" asked the director.

"What about Broadway," echoed chorus girls on a stage in New York.

"Who knows? Maybe Warner Brothers will want to shoot it," suggested the anxious actor to the movie agent.

"In Wabbit season!" yelled Daffy Duck.

"Nah, in Duck season," replied Bugs Bunny.

"Wabbit season!" insisted Daffy.

"Duck Season," munched Bugs.

"Wabbit season!" screamed the Duck.

"Wabbit season!" mimicked the Rabbit.

"Duck season!" triumphed Winnie and Tin Man (but not the real ones!).

"I don't care what season it is, who's taken my carrots?" moaned Elmer from a television shooting at stars hoping for success one way or another. But President Brady was speechless because he had finally realised that no matter what Elmer said, it was the Mouse and not the Rabbit who found diamonds when looking for kinky tails in a vegetable garden.

And after choosing the real pie from Australia, Moby's Mouse prepared two memos for pinning on CEOs, but calling them: Elephant Stories and Kinky Tales: Restoration of Almighty God's blessing for the people of Australia, England, United States, and those countries who were lied to before joining the coalition of the willing to invade Iraq from ...

His Roses and Thorns

ONCERNING THEME RIDES AND HORROR MOVIE type ideas such as say, the Osama Express, a key to prevent train thoughts from flying off their tracks is to have two happy endings. Although, in the true Wonderland it doesn't matter so much because Walt always includes jumbo breaks in His script, so runaway train thoughts tend to stop quickly. But in our world, whilst different a story ends the same way. A Mouse says he thinks Christopher Robbins calls it a rub out. How it works is in Walt's movies since he dislikes steel stories, if a horror scene is included in His script, numbers are stacked against the enemy at disproportionate levels. So Walt is discriminatory, but only at holy rock concerts.

Generally, what happens in the story is the enemies are given a warning, usually in the form of Elephants and Mice; depending on where the kinky tales are of course. But the truth is Walt draws the nightmare first then writes His fairytale. Nevertheless, it's always as if He has the same plot namely, Dumbo's magic has gone, so Christopher Robbins is unable to show Winnie how to water the trees and flowers so the wildlife behaves. And to date things have been rather scary, because as we know Buggs and Daffy crossed over from Warner Brothers and persuaded Bobby and Marty into landing Jumbos on Sesame Street.

However, to make matters worse, on this occasion Elmer also blew a fuse at the shenanigans, which at the time was probably understandable, but still inexcusable just the same. So due to the previous ideas Walt has two endings with a King of Spades story, because apart from His Ivory Points everyone is second. Hence, the theme for a script is called His Thorns will beat Her Roses any day in the game of no trumps, which means wise men know His fairytale is Amazing Grace not hell raising Ace, and that's why He calls it Heaven.

But if the actors do not say their lines and/or follow His script; their fairytale is only sadness in a windswept field because the scene is a mountainous desert, except for a lonely tree that has no fruit, only snaky branches. Or the dead tree of life if one wants to be biblical. Nevertheless, hanging from the tree's branch that sits over the headstone next to its trunk is a noose and nothing else except hot winds, shifting sands, and an oily well where once they preached. It happens because actors in the field have failed to put a brake on their train of thought, or understood they don't use His Crown to encourage steel tails with neon lights to fly into New York stories.

And the scene is set because when Dumbo loses His magic, the King of Spades is visible. So He lets Judas out of a noose to meet with the disciples again. Afterwards, to offer the Devil a tempting deal the King uses His Thorny Crown to attract Lucifer and the atheists. The deal is if Lucifer helps, Jesus allows him to keep all of the peanuts laying in a Potter's field because Judas wants empty shells with no hearts for his plot.

Next, as the Osama Express speeds towards its destination a wall of Mice form a barrier across the tracks. However, they sit behind a huge arrangement of instruments waiting for the rattle and hum from the drums that beat to rock music; which have flashing lights with fireworks that shoot stars onto the stage.

Only the horns from the band aren't made of brass, and strings from their guitars amplify notes the size of Texas, that scream songs of Sunday Bloody Sunday and Allah Come Back all over the field. Nonetheless, the sad part is the Ace doesn't care for the sweet surrender of forgiveness has gone, because like Graceland's Elvis, Almighty God has disappeared. But upon leaving His message was, "to find logic, they need to realise a betrayal means Pilate tales are evident, Judas was hanged, Barabbas was freed, roses have withered, rocks have moved, and His Invisible Hands have appeared." Therefore, a reason for His appearance wasn't for personal gratification, rather, it was a reminder that we are not alone and we are not the authors in our story because God is.

Thus, in God's fairytale there is room for only one statue. And He was the reason why I chose not to be her friend for after meeting her, I thought God wasn't in her heart and she was just a body painted in gold, but paid for by an oilfield. Personally, I find that type of statue difficult to have faith in for God is the air I breathe. And I believe people are only lonely since they have no faith. The frightened have little faith, foolish can't find faith, those who crave attention can't see faith, people who cry thunder can't hear faith; whilst others with excuses ignore faith.

However, personally I have no excuse for ignoring God, but a hundred for not hearing politicians. And whilst my views may not be popular, because I feel they make sense more than anything else, they are my foremost thought. For example, I realised how attractive she was without noticing a physical appearance, and understood how intelligent she was without pondering academic achievements. And I knew how responsible she was without considering a mortgage. Then after allowing for rejection, I understood how kind she had been.

But if she had trusted nature she would have found that when we first met, I wasn't hoping for friendship because my heart said, "Perhaps this angel's beauty comes from within." As I have found, when others hope they fail to realise this was never the answer in friendship, because it is similar to a rose. So the reason for flowers is hope because compared to thorns, roses only bloom for the short term.

You see, when nature is right roses bloom, but after pruning all that's left are thorns. And for reasons of a florist in us throughout centuries man has harvested nature's fruits, because whilst we know the petals won't last, nothing says it better than roses. But if she knew our habits made us this way what would nature do, or does nature make us harvest so we feel right, rather than hope we are right?

Frequently, world leaders have a balance of power in this situation because Sheep can't guess themselves. But sometimes, like a symbol some leaders are bound by a stance until they are covered in roses; never knowing if a new statue has replaced them or not. Meanwhile, thorns on the outside continue to prosper because they have faith in the beat of Mother Nature's heart, which comes from the wings of a Butterfly, or those of a Bee. And when I last heard the wise men talk, they said at the heart of nature was God, so from time to time He must be a Woman?

Even so, some women are like the roses I have sent her. They are beautiful, but when I last saw an angel there is no comparison as to who was the better of the two. Although, at the time of describing her I couldn't find more beautiful than flowers because it was the best nature could do.

And surprisingly, when paying the florist it seemed her thoughts also reflected my mind, for when she put a coin in my hand she smiled and said, "You never know your luck in a regatta, because sometimes it rains and sometimes it doesn't." However, after nodding with agreement I noticed that one side of her coin was stamped with His Thorns and the other, His Tale.

And amazingly, as I stepped out onto the pavement from beneath cloudy skies I thought I caught the shadow of an Angel, carrying roses, but heading north to meet Judas. Although, it seemed those bouquets were for the other tails, whose hearts were made from diamonds, but cut with tears for fears, by the rose coloured glass of New York and the Jumbo blades with...

Invisible Hands

Australia's an acrobat and God wants the world however, a Jack doesn't want to be an Angel of Harlem. And whilst it might be a beautiful day, desire isn't better than the real thing because Ireland wants to find Jesus. But they still haven't found what they're looking for so perhaps in a little while Allah will move in mysterious ways. And he isn't New Year's Day or a zoo station with a miner's passion although, like a fly he went to stay in a land faraway so close. But if wild honey's the sweetest thing until the end of the world then what happens on the day when love comes to town? England had the signs for the streets with no name although, she can't find who rode the wild horses with or without a new star. And he wasn't the fourth of July or a sort of home coming, but it wasn't bad because from the ashes of an Indian summer sky Elvis solved a puzzle. So the Queen found rain from MLK because in their country His star on the promenade has the unforgettable fire. Therefore, Grace sent a wire so Liberty could throw her arms around His missing Mice, because the President knows her thoughts are love is blindness and not everybody wants to rule the world. And if Two Towers weren't so cruel or in the name of Allah's ring, then like ultra violet there were bullets in the blue sky because Jesus is a rock that can't sing. But when the Jumbos overlooked one tree hill Liberty's cry didn't fail to reach him running to stand still. Born from a red hill mining town Jersusa didn't trip on their wires because his choice was a tree without elevation. Then to mine a heart so freedom could walk on wild honey she needed a card to play her game, but the Joshua tree alone in the desert was a Spade. And whilst the black rose was lonesome in a way, he wasn't to be Francine's wild honey in a peanut bar. So Achtung Baby had a dance not once, but twice with a diamond lance that was stolen from Jumbo blades held by Grace and His Invisible Hands. Then a game with false claims began and the President proved that he was the best against the statue with a star. And Saddam become no challenge like rattle and hum when his statues faced Sunday bloody Sunday from Grace's gun. Although, we don't know if God's here anymore because the truth wasn't a reason for the Gulf War. And whilst they saw oil beneath the land at the same time there wasn't an excuse for the statues with their skeleton closets and the Jumbo plan. Hence, the real trumps are in freedom's cards, Master Jaques, because an Aussie sling doesn't march to the tune of a club. And Mice are tired of kinky tales flown with iron intellects, but not the gold album that sells without a voice because he can hear music and understand the word God. However, would it be unwise if an Australian said that there's room in his heart for Amazing Grace instead? And yes we know terrorists are clowns and with their tails two burnt down. But weren't you shaken when you heard the screams as Two Towers crashed and it was no dream? Or was that Liberty with a tear in her eye when she saw her sons and daughters jump to die? So please say we fight in the name of their sad days. And keep singing Bono, Edge, Adam, and Larry, since they haven't understood dear God please. He loves our music, but at the end of a day the world has a troublesome past, so we should lose our cards printed in black and stained with red glass. Although, perhaps it's best to see a Judge for terrorists to understand that God's one and only statue is Amazing Grace with Invisible Hands, Amen. **Please save their shattered hearts Almighty God; and thanks to U2 …**

Yours faithfully and to be continued

From a Jack to a King

With no Wedding Ring

www.ingramcontent.com/pod-product-compliance
Lightning Source LLC
Chambersburg PA
CBHW031253250726
48655CB00005B/2202